MUSIC THEORY AND ARRANGING TECHNIQUES FOR FOLK HARPS

by SYLVIA WOODS

THANKS TO:
Suzanne Balderston, Cyndee Crane, Judy Diaz, Debby Friou,
Anne Geldin, Suzanne Guldimann, Lynn Lockwood, Vicki Pellom,
Conway Snyder, and Gina Wilson.

Cover Art by Steve Duglas
Music typeset by Robert Lau

Printed by Delta Lithograph, California, USA

All arrangements by Sylvia Woods

P.O. Box 29521, Los Angeles, California 90029 USA

ISBN 0-936661-02-X

Table Of Contents

Introduction

Did you ever want to play a particular piece on your harp, but you couldn't find a harp arrangement of it? Or maybe you found a nice arrangement, but it was in the wrong key? Or perhaps you picked up a guitar book and wondered how you could play the songs on your harp? Or maybe you have decided to learn more about music so you'll be a better musician.

If you answered "yes" to any of these questions, this book is for you. In this book I will teach you the music theory and arranging techniques you'll need to play out of non-harp music books, and to make your own harp arrangements.

Don't let the words "music theory" and "arranging" scare you. Contrary to what anyone may have told you in the past, these are not difficult subjects if you take them one step at a time. And that is what we will do in this book. Start with Chapter 1, follow all of the instructions carefully, and continue through the book. Before you know it, you'll be making your own arrangements.

I have tried to put a variety of pieces in this book so that there will be some to suit almost any taste. In sections where there are lots of pieces, you don't necessarily need to play them all. Just remember that the more practice and experience you gain as you go along, the better your arrangements will be. As you are playing through the pieces in this book, mark the ones you particularly like so you can refer to them later. In the more advanced chapters you'll want to go back to some of the earlier pieces and "spice them up" with your newly acquired arranging techniques.

I am assuming that you already know the basics of harp playing before you use this book. You don't have to be advanced, but you should know the basic playing techniques, including placing and fingering. As in normal harp playing, all chords of 3 or more notes in this book should be played "slightly broken" (i.e. "rolled").

Throughout most of this book, you should have your harp tuned to the key of C (with no sharps or flats). If you have been playing in my "Teach Yourself to Play the Folk Harp" book, this is how your harp has been tuned.

Even if you have had previous music theory background, I suggest that you start reading at Chapter 1, instead of skipping ahead. It will be a good review for you, and will get you used to the way I approach things and the nomenclature that I use. You may find that I come from a different viewpoint than you've encountered before, which may show you ideas in a different light. And who knows, you may learn something you never knew before.

Periodically throughout the book I have printed blank staff paper for your use. You may want to buy a book of staff paper, as well, to write out some of your ideas and arrangements. This paper can be purchased at most sheet music stores, and some stationery stores.

Have fun with this book. Don't make it so serious that you miss the joy you can obtain by making the music your own. Remember that there are lots of different ways to make arrangements, and you'll develop a style of your own. Don't be intimidated by someone else's expertise. Just go at your own pace, and take it step by step. The more arrangements you do, the better they will become. All it takes is practice and a little imagination. Enjoy yourself: arranging is lots of fun!

Feel free to write to me and let me know how you're doing. I love to hear from all of you. My address is: Sylvia Woods Harp Center, P.O. Box 29521, Los Angeles, CA 90029.

Chapter 1 - Major Chords

If you are like most people (myself included), you probably just turned to this page and started reading, without reading the "Introduction" first. If so, please go back and read the "Introduction" so I'm sure we're all starting together. Thank you!

The first step in arranging is learning to play and identify various chords. Chords are groups of notes that are played together. For example, a C chord is made up of the notes C, E, and G. Play these three notes on your harp with your 3rd finger on C, your 2nd finger on E, and your thumb on G. Notice that you skip one string between each finger, i.e., you don't play the D and the F. This is called a C major chord. Play C chords like this in several octaves on your harp. Say the names of the notes as you play so that you learn which notes are in the chord. Try to get your hand used to this position of skipping a string between each note.

Let's try another chord: G. The spacing is just the same as for the C chord, you'll skip one string between each finger. Place your 3rd finger on G, your 2nd finger on B, and your thumb on D. This is a G major chord. Practice it in several octaves on your harp until you feel comfortable with it, saying the names of the notes as you play them.

Practice going back and forth between the C chord and the G chord. Play the C chord, then the G, and then back to the C, etc. Sometimes make the G chord higher than the C, and sometimes make it lower. By the way, you should practice all of these exercises with both hands.

Now we'll try playing a few simple tunes that use these two chords: C and G. Play the melody with your right hand and the chords with your left whenever the chord name is written. Notice that generally the chord comes on the first beat of each measure (although this is not always the case). You should play the pieces like this:

CLEMENTINE

But through this book, you will see it notated like this:

CLEMENTINE - CHORD NAMES

This is played just like the first example. The right hand plays the melody, and the left hand reads the chord names.

Now try another American tune, "Down In The Valley". Play it the same way you played "Clementine", with the right hand playing the melody, and the left hand playing the chords. Notice that you'll play a chord on the first beat of each measure even when the melody note is tied.

DOWN IN THE VALLEY

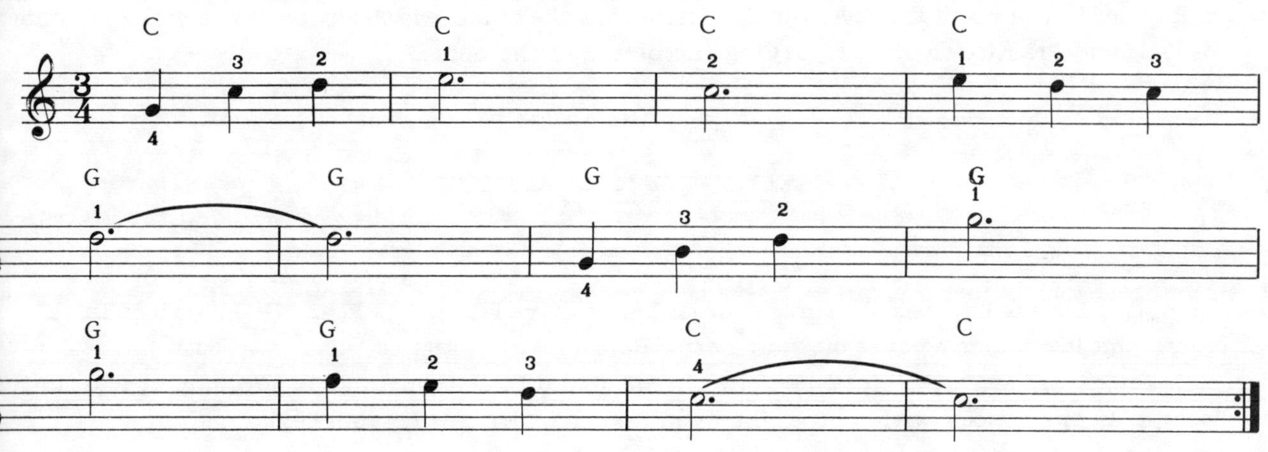

In these next two French pieces, "Sur La Pont D'Avignon" and "Allouette", the chords are sometimes played in the middle of the measure as well as on the first beat. So, play the chords whenever a chord name is written.

SUR LA PONT D'AVIGNON

ALLOUETTE

If we add one more chord, we greatly increase the number of songs we can play. So, let's try an major chord. The notes are F, A, and C. Notice that the spacing is the same as the other two chord we learned. Practice this chord, saying the names of the notes.

Practice moving between the three chords that we have learned: C, F, and G. Play them in variou orders and in various octaves on your harp. Remember to practice them with both hands.

"Farewell To Tarwathie" just uses two chords: C and F. Once again (and throughout most of thi book), play the melody with your right hand and the chords with your left.

FAREWELL TO TARWATHIE

Here are some tunes using all three chords: C, F and G. If your harp has enough strings, experiment with starting on the C chord and either going *UP* to the F or G chord or going *DOWN* to the F or G. See which one you like better in each instance. Sometimes going up will sound better, and sometimes going down will sound better.

If you run out of room for the left hand on any of these pieces (this may happen if you only have an octave below middle C on your harp), try playing the melody an octave higher than written, which will give you more room for the chords.

"Early One Morning" is from England, and "I Know My Love" is Irish.

EARLY ONE MORNING

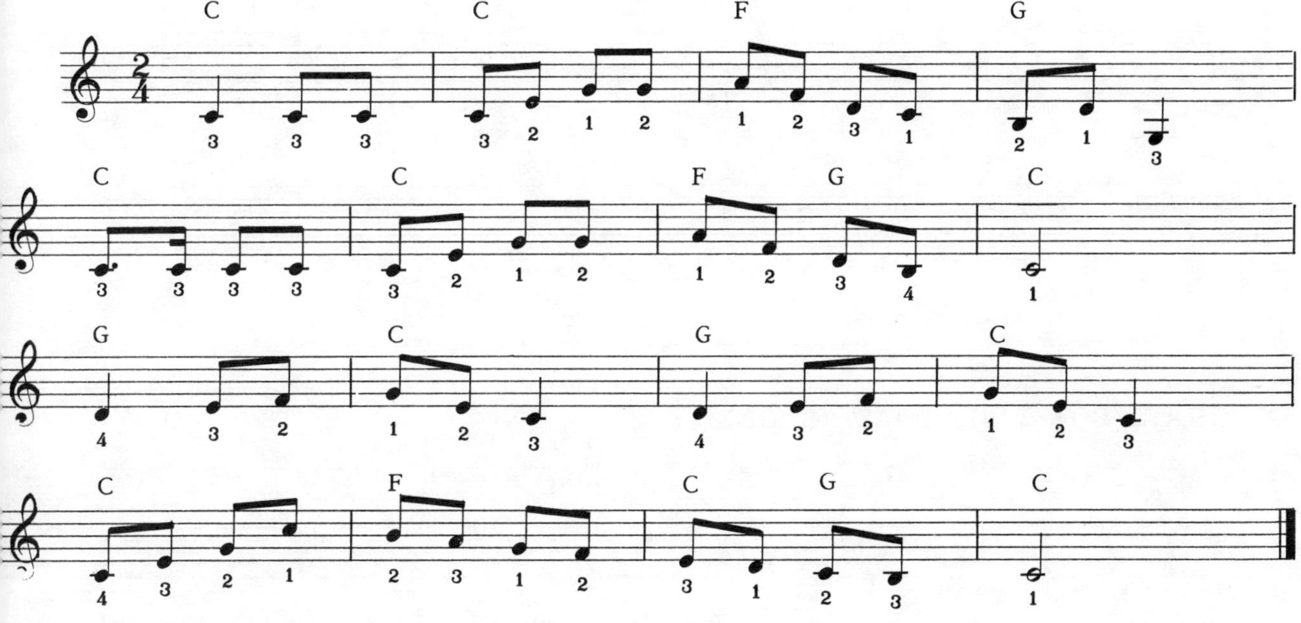

I KNOW MY LOVE

KUM BA YAH

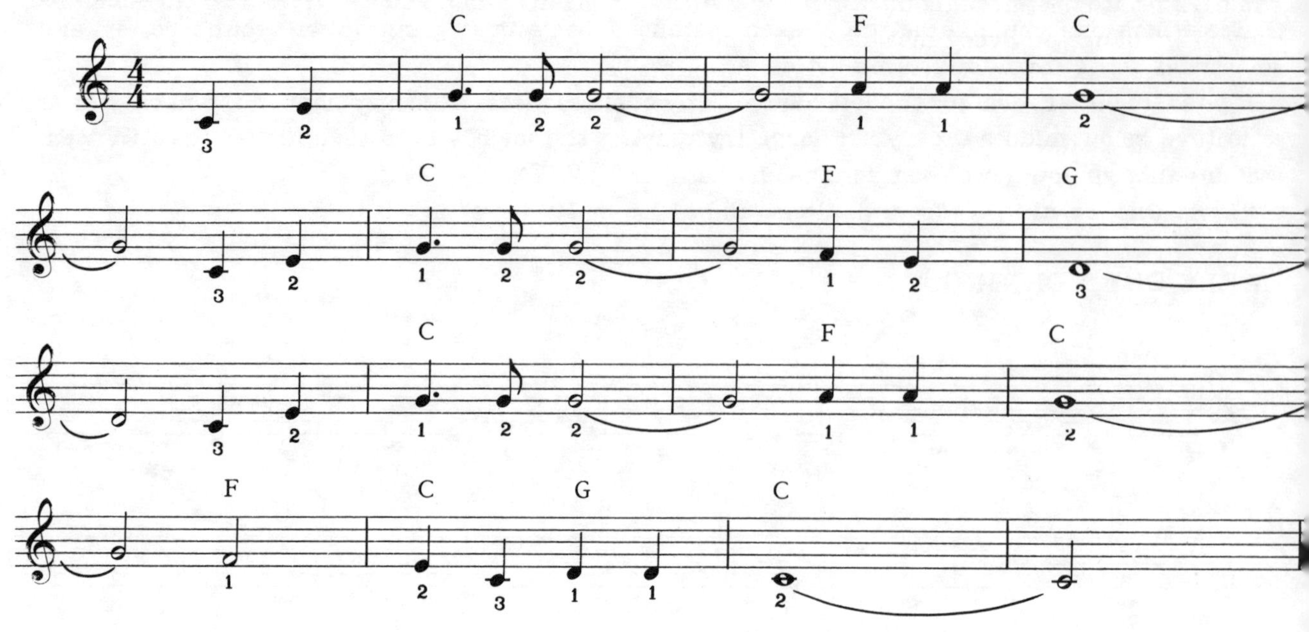

MICHAEL ROW YOUR BOAT ASHORE

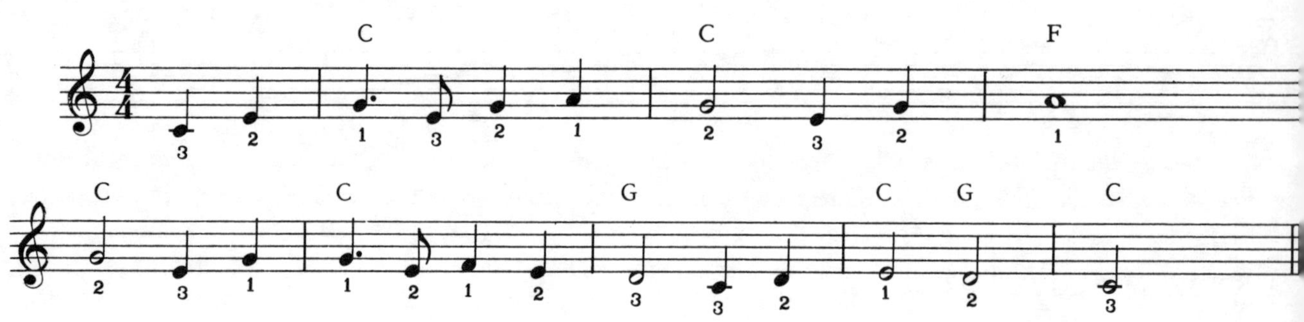

NOBODY KNOWS THE TROUBLE I'VE SEEN

In "Silent Night", notice that each chord lasts for two measures. You only have to play it once, and then let it ring throughout the two measures. It is only when you get to the last three chords that they change on every measure.

SILENT NIGHT

These three chords that we have learned (C, F, and G) are all called major chords. Although they start on different notes, they each have similar sounds. One way to tell whether or not a chord is a major chord is to try to sing the first 3 notes of "Michael Row Your Boat Ashore" to the three notes of the chord. For example, play the notes of a C chord and sing the first 3 notes of "Michael" like this:

This sounds fine. That means that the C chord is major. Try it with the G chord and the F chord, and you'll find that they work, too.

And so, the C, F, and G chords are all major.

Chapter 2 - Minor Chords

There is another common type of chord: a "minor" chord. Minor chords sound different from the major chords. Many people say they sound "sadder" or "more melancholy".

Using the same configuration we used on the major chords (skipping one string between each finger), play an A chord on your harp (A, C, E). Can you hear that it sounds different from the other chords we have played? Play it again. It is a minor chord: "A minor". If you try to sing "Michael Row" on the first 3 notes, it won't work. Try it.

Can you hear that the second note sounds wrong? That is because the chord is minor, and not major.

Play A minor chords up and down your harp, getting used to the sound of the chord, and saying the names of the notes as you go.

Let's try two other minor chords: D minor (D, F, A) and E minor (E, G, B). Practice these until you feel comfortable with them, saying the names of the chords and the notes. Listen to the similarities between the three minor chords.

The shorthand way of indicating a minor chord is to use a small "m" like this: Dm. In some books, they use a capital letter for the name of the chord when it is major, and a small letter for the minor chord, like this: "D" for D major, "d" for d minor. In this book we use the more common "Dm" to indicate a D minor chord, and just "D" to indicate D major.

Practice moving between these three chords: Am, Dm and Em. Play them in various orders until you feel comfortable with them.

The Negro spiritual, "Wayfaring Stranger", uses all three minor chords: Am, Dm and Em.

WAYFARING STRANGER

This old English ballad uses all three minor chords.

THE TREES THEY GROW HIGH

Many pieces use a combination of minor chords and major chords. In these next pieces you'll play mostly minor chords, with some major chords thrown in for "variety". "Bold Fenian Men" is based on an old Irish Air, "Our Ship Did Sail" is from the Isle of Man, and "My Love's in Germany" is Scottish.

BOLD FENIAN MEN

OUR SHIP DID SAIL

MY LOVE'S IN GERMANY

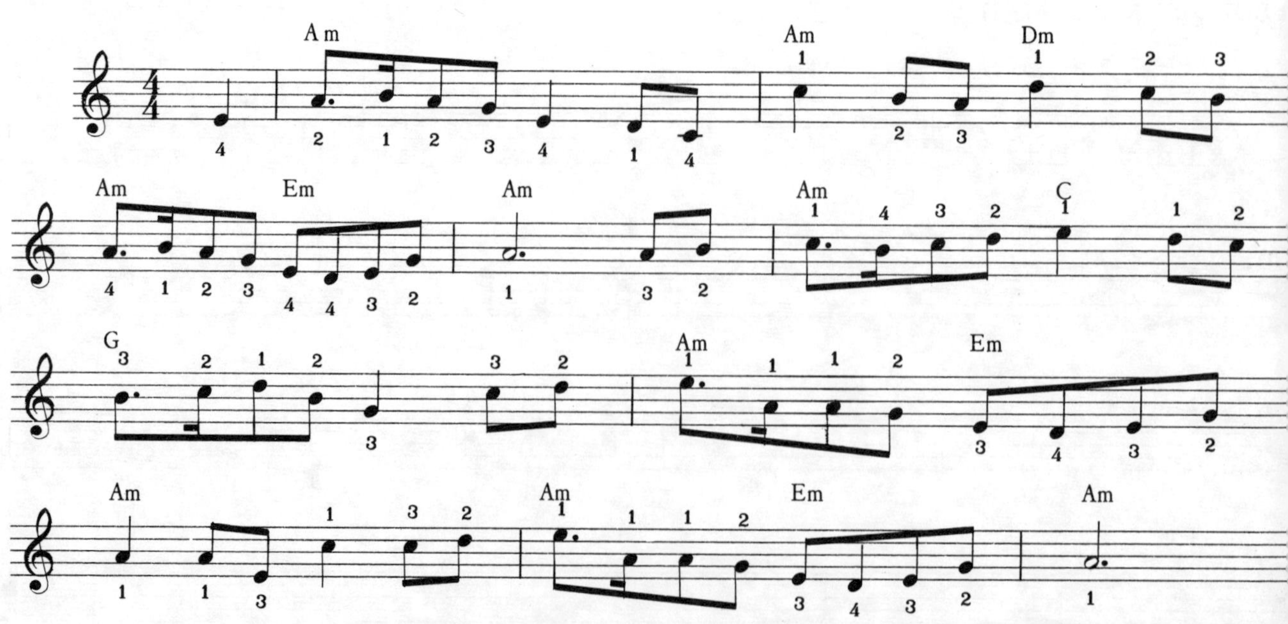

The Negro spiritual, "Swing Low, Sweet Chariot", uses mostly major chords, with a few Am chords for "spice".

SWING LOW, SWEET CHARIOT

Look at the chords in the 5th and 6th measures of "Hame, Hame, Hame" (which means "Home, Home, Home" in Scots Gaelic). Notice the nice downward progression of chords: Am, G, F, Em, Dm. This is also repeated in the 9th and 10th measures. So be sure you start these progressions with a high enough Am chord to give you room to go down all the way to the Dm.

HAME, HAME, HAME

Sometimes in the lower register of the harp, chords sound better if you leave out the middle note. For example, if you play this low Am chord here:

Am

it can sound a bit "muddy", especially if your harp rings a lot in the lower octaves. Now try playing it leaving out the middle note (leave out the C) like this:

It seems to "clean up" the sound a bit. Try this in "The Famine Song" from Ireland. Sometimes you can play a higher Am (around "middle C") and use all three notes, and sometimes play it an octave lower and leave out the C:

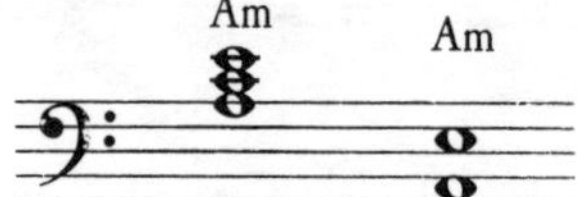

THE FAMINE SONG

"Brave Wolfe" is a song from Canada. Notice that on the first beat of lines 2, 3, and 4 and the very last measure, the chord is played on the first beat even though the melody note is tied. Three of these chords are Am, and are great candidates for playing on the lower part of the harp, leaving out the middle note, as we just did on "The Famine Song".

BRAVE WOLFE

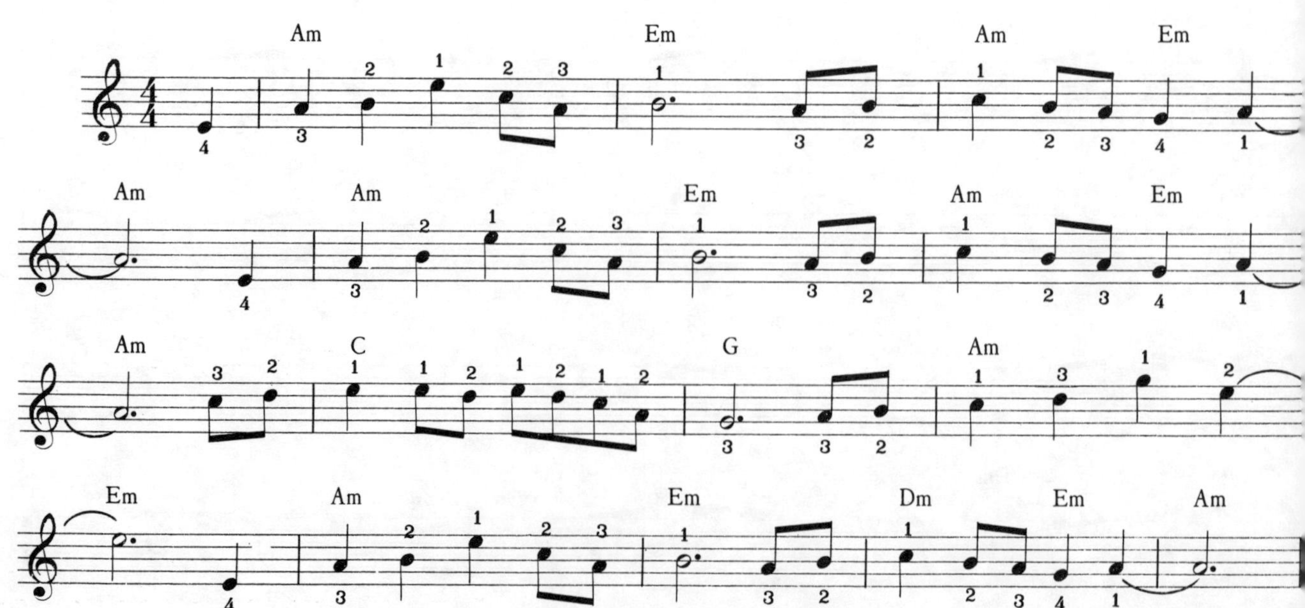

Long, sustained notes like you hear on a bagpipe are called drones. The Am chords in the first line of the French song "The Mowers", create this same effect. Notice that I didn't write a chord on the second and fourth measures. That is because you can just let the Am chord ring. If you want to put in Am chords on the first beats of those measures, too, that's fine. It is up to you. The same goes for the Em chord at the end of the second line.

THE MOWERS

Another piece that sounds good with a drone-like accompaniment is the Scottish song "Who'll Be King But Charlie". The drone effect comes in at the beginning and where there are a lot of Am chords in a row. Try using either a regular Am chord around middle C or an octave lower than that leaving out the C, as we did on "The Famine Song".

WHO'LL BE KING BUT CHARLIE

Chapter 3 - Intervals

An interval is the distance between two notes. For example, the distance between one C note and the next higher C note is an octave, that is, it is an interval of an octave. The word octave comes from the root "oct", meaning "8" (as in octagon, octopus, etc.). If you start on C, counting C as "1", and count up to the next C, you'll count 8 notes: C=1, D=2, E=3, F=4, G=5, A=6, B=7, C=8. So, the interval between C and C is an "octave".

Let's look at a C chord and see what intervals it contains. From the C to the E of the chord is an interval of a 3rd: (C=1, D=2, E=3). From the C to the G of the chord is an interval of a 5th: (C=1, D=2, E=3, F=4, G=5).

The three notes in a chord all have names, which makes it easier to talk about them. The note that the chord is named after is called the "root". For example, in a C chord, the C note is the "root"; in an F chord the F is the root; in an Am chord the A is the root, etc.

As we learned above, the interval between the root and the next note of a chord is an interval of a 3rd (in a C chord it is an interval of a 3rd between C and E). Therefore, this middle note (the E) is called the "3rd" of the chord. Following the same logic, the highest note of the chord (the G in the C chord) is called the "5th" of the chord.

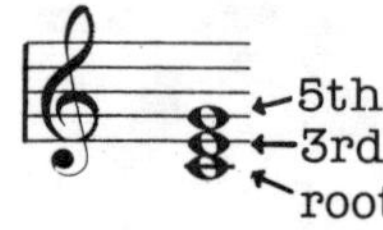

And so to summarize, each chord is made up of a root note, a 3rd, and a 5th. Here are a few examples:

F chord: F = root, A = 3rd, C = 5th
G chord: G = root, B = 3rd, D = 5th
A minor chord: A = root, C = 3rd, E = 5th
D minor chord: D = root, F = 3rd, A = 5th

Play various chords on your harp, saying "root, 3rd, 5th", until you are sure you understand it.

It is important that you learn to recognize all the intervals, and so here's a little quiz for you. Below each two-note chord, write the name of the interval. For example, the first chord is an interval of a 3rd between the A and C, the second one is a 5th between E and B, the third one is a 2nd between G and A, etc. When you're done, you can check your answers in the appendix.

INTERVAL EXERCISE

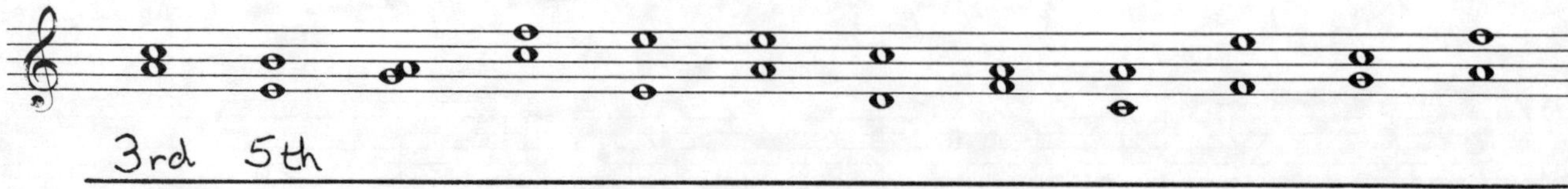

Chapter 4 - Inversions

All the chords we have learned so far have been in the "root position", meaning that the root of the chord has been the lowest note played. For example, the root note of a C chord is a C note, and when we play a C chord, we put the C as the lowest note (3rd finger), and then the third of the chord and the fifth of the chord are on top (2nd finger and thumb).

However, you don't always have to play a C chord in that order. You can mix up the three notes AS LONG AS YOU ONLY PLAY THE THREE NOTES THAT ARE IN A C CHORD: C, E, and G. And so, if you play E, G, and C like this:

C

that is a C chord, too, because it has the three notes of a C chord. Although the "bottom" 2 notes might make it look like it is an Em chord because of the E and the G, it can't be an Em, because it has a C instead of a B. The only chord that this can be is a C chord, in a different order. This is called a FIRST INVERSION C CHORD. We inverted it once (or turned it upside-down once) by moving the C from the bottom of the chord to the top. Play this first inversion C chord on your harp. Notice that there is a skip of one string between your 3rd and 2nd fingers, but there is a skip of TWO STRINGS between your 2nd finger and your thumb. Practice this inversion until it feels comfortable.

All first inversion chords have the same spacing as the one we just learned: a skip of one string between the 3rd finger and the 2nd, and a skip of 2 strings between the 2nd and the thumb. Your thumb is now playing the root note of the chord. Let's try some more first inversion chords. (To make the chords easy to read and compare, I'll be writing them in the treble clef throughout this book, even though you'll generally be playing them with the left hand in the lower part of the harp.)

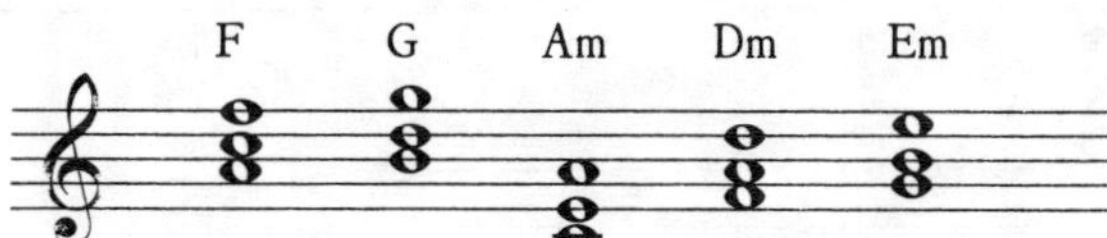

Practice these first inversions. Get your hands used to this spacing of one skip and then two skips. Think about the notes and the chords you are playing. It is very important to know which notes are in which chords.

SECOND INVERSION CHORDS

To get our first inversion C chord, we inverted the chord once by moving the C note from the bottom of the chord to the top, which placed the E note on the bottom. What do you suppose a second inversion C chord is? A second inversion inverts it one more time, so that now the G is on the bottom, making the chord G, C, E.

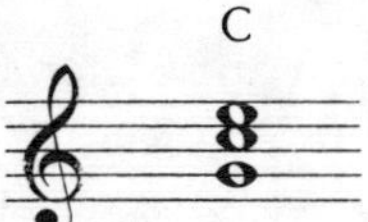

This is still a C chord, since it has the three notes of a C chord in it, but it is just in a different order. Even though it has a G on the bottom, it couldn't be a G chord, because a G chord needs a B and a D, and shouldn't have a C or an E. The only possible chord it could be is a C chord in the second inversion.

Play this second inversion C chord again (G, C, E). Notice the spacing of this chord. This time it has a skip of TWO strings between the 3rd finger and the 2nd finger, and a skip of ONE between the 2nd finger and the thumb. All second inversion chords have this spacing.

Practice all these second inversion chords.

F G Am Dm Em

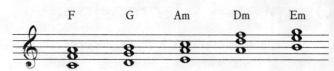

There is a shorthand way of writing down inversions, so that you remember which inversion of the chord you want to play. This is the way music is written for studio musicians who play on record albums and movie and TV soundtracks. The shorthand notation is like this: the chord/the name of the lowest note. For example, if they wanted a second inversion C chord, they would write C/G, which means a C chord with a G on the bottom, or the notes G, C and E. F/A means an F chord with an A on the bottom (a first inversion F chord). Em/B means an E minor chord with a B on the bottom (a second inversion E minor chord).

Here are some examples of the shorthand and the notes that they signify. (It doesn't matter which octave you play them in; I've just written them in the most convenient place to keep the notes on the staff.)

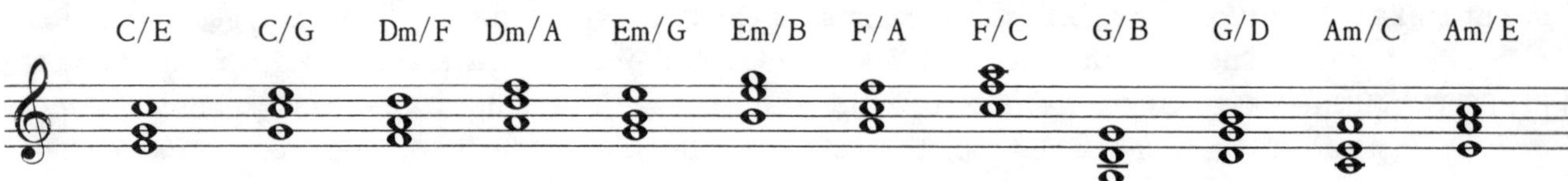

Here are two quizzes for you. In the first one, write the shorthand names above the chords. In the second, write the notes of the chords on the staff. Check your answers in the Appendix.

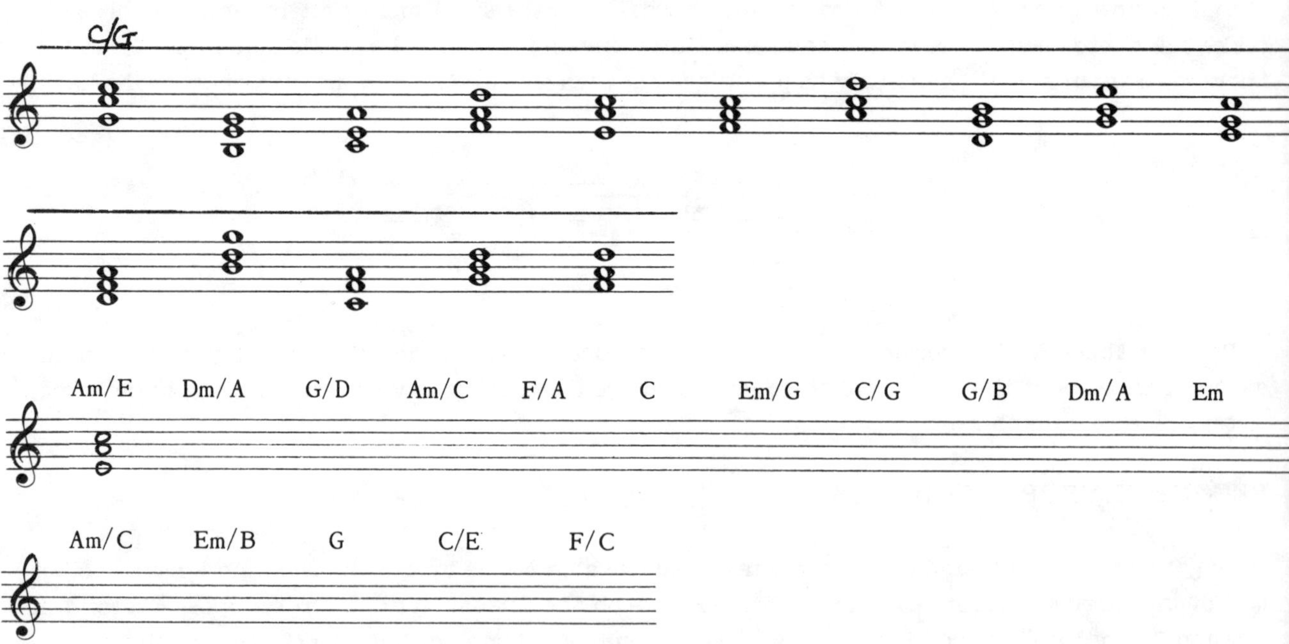

Now that you know your chords and their inversions, you can practice them like this. Take one chord, a C chord for example, and play it in the root position, then move up to the first inversion, then the second inversion, then up to the root again, etc., as shown below. Practice all chords like this. BE CAREFUL TO ONLY PLAY THE CORRECT THREE NOTES FOR EACH CHORD. DON'T ACCIDENTALLY CHANGE A NOTE. For example, if you are playing a C chord, only use the C, E, and G notes. Be sure you are playing inversions, not other chords.

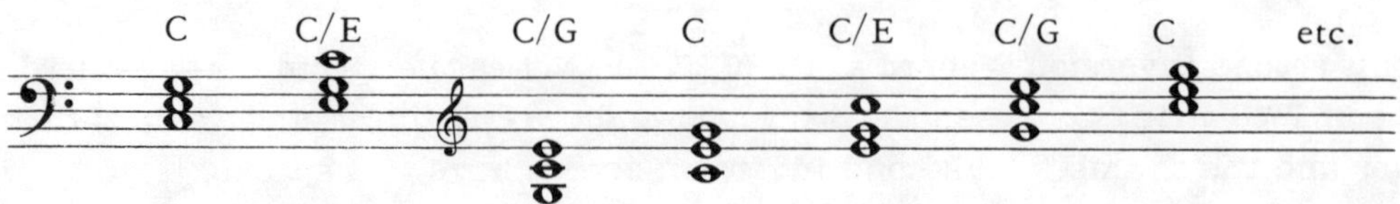

VARYING INVERSIONS ON REPEATED CHORDS

"Why are inversions necessary?" you may ask. There are many reasons we will discuss throughout this book. One is that, especially on small harps, you often run out of strings to be able to play all the chords in the root position without falling off the bottom of the harp, or getting in the way of the melody.

For example, if your harp has only one octave below middle C, and you try to play "Lavender's Blue", you'll run into trouble in the 7th and 8th measures. If you play the G chord in the root position, the top note of the chord (your left thumb) is on the same string that you should be playing with your right hand for the melody. You can't just move the chord down an octave, because you'll run out of strings on your small harp. So, the solution is to play the G chord in the 2nd inversion, with a D on the bottom (D, G, B). On the music for "Lavender's Blue" below, write in the shorthand for an inversion on those two G chords. That is, write /D after the G chords, making them G/D. Now play the piece like this and see how it sounds.

LAVENDER'S BLUE

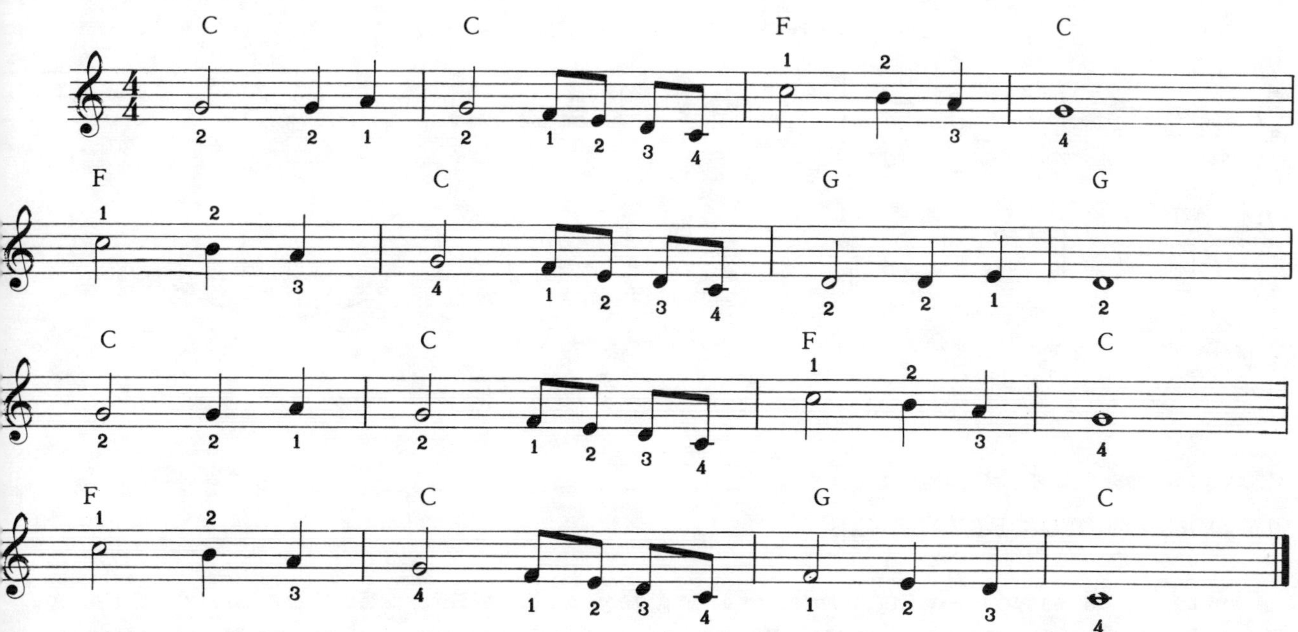

A second reason for using inversions is to give variety to a repeated chord. For example, notice that the first two chords of "Lavender's Blue" are both C chords. Try keeping the first C chord in the root position, but make the second C chord a first inversion (C/E). Write this C/E in both the second measure and the tenth measure. Play the piece again and see how you changed the sound.

Sometimes a piece has one chord that keeps repeating for a very long time. This can tend to get a bit boring. However, if you vary the inversions you use, it will sound much more pleasing.

Let's try this with "Silent Night". Play chords on each measure instead of every other measure as we did earlier, and change inversions. I'll get you started with a few inversions, but then you can write in your own for the rest of the piece.

SILENT NIGHT

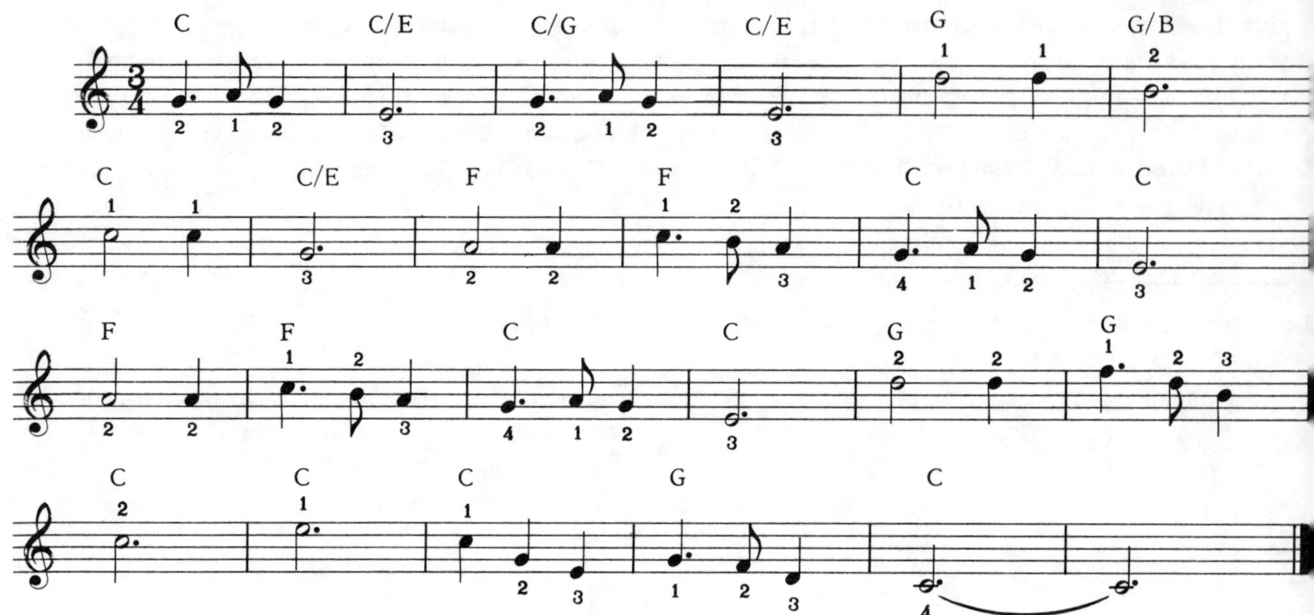

INVERSIONS FOR BASS LINES

Another good reason for using inversions is to give you a more interesting bass line. "But I'm not even using a bass line!", you may say. Well, I hate to disillusion you, but you have been playing a bass line in all the pieces we have played so far. Keep reading, and I'll explain.

The melody, of course, is the most important line. It is generally the highest line, as well. Whether you're consciously aware of it or not, the lowest note you play becomes a bass line, and is perceived as such by the ear. And so, the inversion you decide to use will greatly influence (in fact it will dictate) your bass line.

Let's use the first line of the Irish tune "Gypsy Rover" as an example. Play it with all the chords in the root position.

GYPSY ROVER - FIRST LINE

e bass line you just played was: C, G, C, G, C, G, C, G. Even if you add some variety by sometimes .ng *UP* to the G from the C chord and sometimes going *DOWN* to the G from the C chord, it still ;s a bit boring.

Now try the piece again, using the inversions indicated.

'PSY ROVER - FIRST LINE

his time, your bass line was much more interesting: C, D, E, D, C, D, E, G. You were able to play all he chords close by without having to move around a lot on the harp, and it sounded more musical.

You can even try adding extra notes in the bass to "fill in the skips". For example, if you look at ne last measure in this line we've been working on, the bass skips from E up to G. You can add an F ote between them to fill in the skip, like this:

Now you're ready for all four lines of "Gypsy Rover" using chord inversions. Notice that the hords are played on the first and third beats of each measure. In the next-to-the-last measures on oth the second and fourth lines of this piece, the C/E chord is played on the first beat, and the F hord is played on the *THIRD* beat, even though there is no melody note played on that beat.

'YPSY ROVER

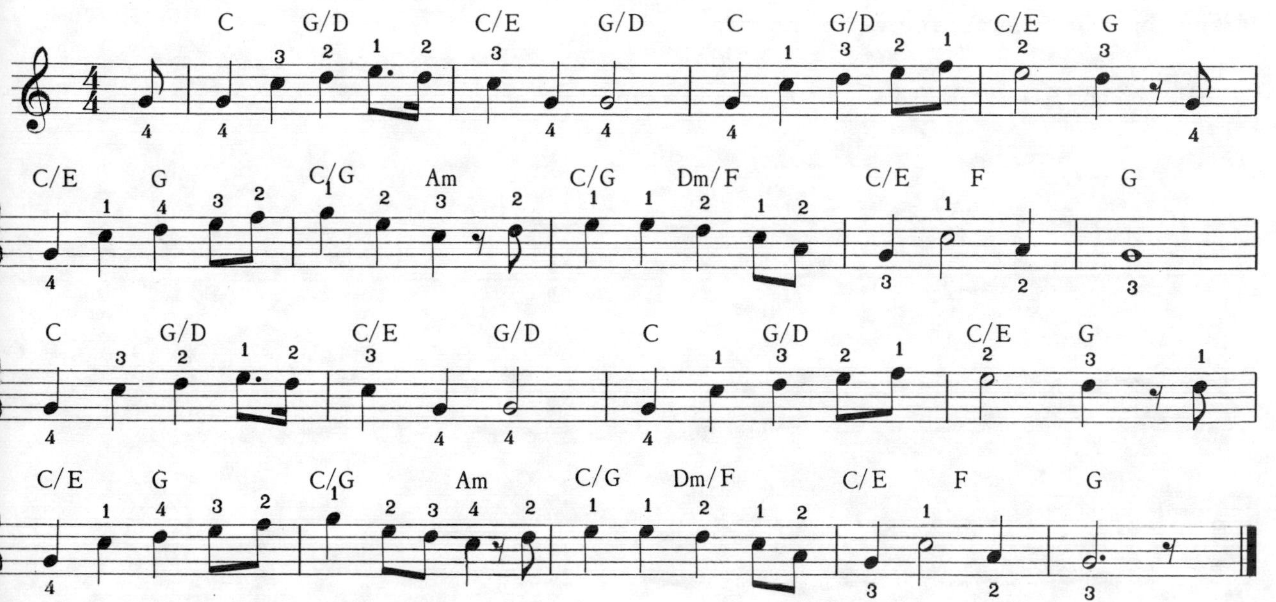

And so, if you think about what bass line your chord inversions are forming, your arrangemen will be much more exciting. As you can see, the better you know your chords and inversions, th easier this will be.

Let's try another example. Play the last two lines of "When I Was Single", without using any in versions. Now try it with the inversions indicated. Listen to the nice descending bass line create by the inversions: F, E, D, C. Now play the whole piece with the inversions. Experiment with di ferent inversions on the second line, and when you've decided what you like, write them in.

WHEN I WAS SINGLE

The next-to-the-last measure of the popular Scottish song "Comin' Thro' The Rye" is another goo example of a descending bass line formed by inversions. Add your own inversions to the rest of th piece: experiment with different inversions, decide which ones you like in the context of the piec and the other chords, and write them in.

COMIN' THRO' THE RYE

In "MacPherson's Farewell" I used a descending bass line, and also some ascending bass lines in the last 4 measures. Once again, add your own inversions throughout the rest of the piece.

MAC PHERSON'S FAREWELL

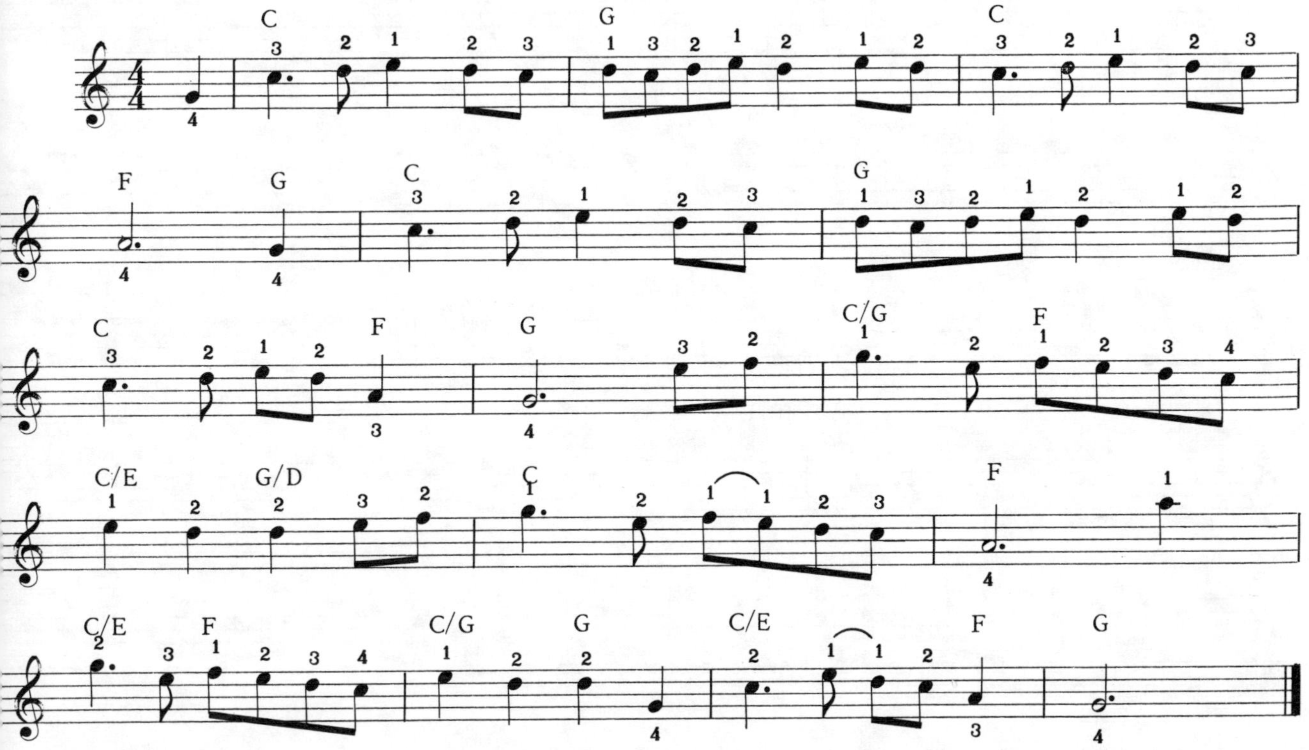

I have included suggestions for some of the inversions in the following pieces. Try them out, change them if you'd like, and add your own. Don't be afraid to experiment and make the arrangement yours.

"Annie Laurie" and "Loch Lomond" are from Scotland. "The Fanaid Grove" and "The Wind From the West" are both Irish, but "The Leaving of Liverpool" is claimed by both Ireland and England. "Steal Away" is a Negro spiritual, and "The Simple Birth" is a Christmas song from the Netherlands.

ANNIE LAURIE

LOCH LOMOND

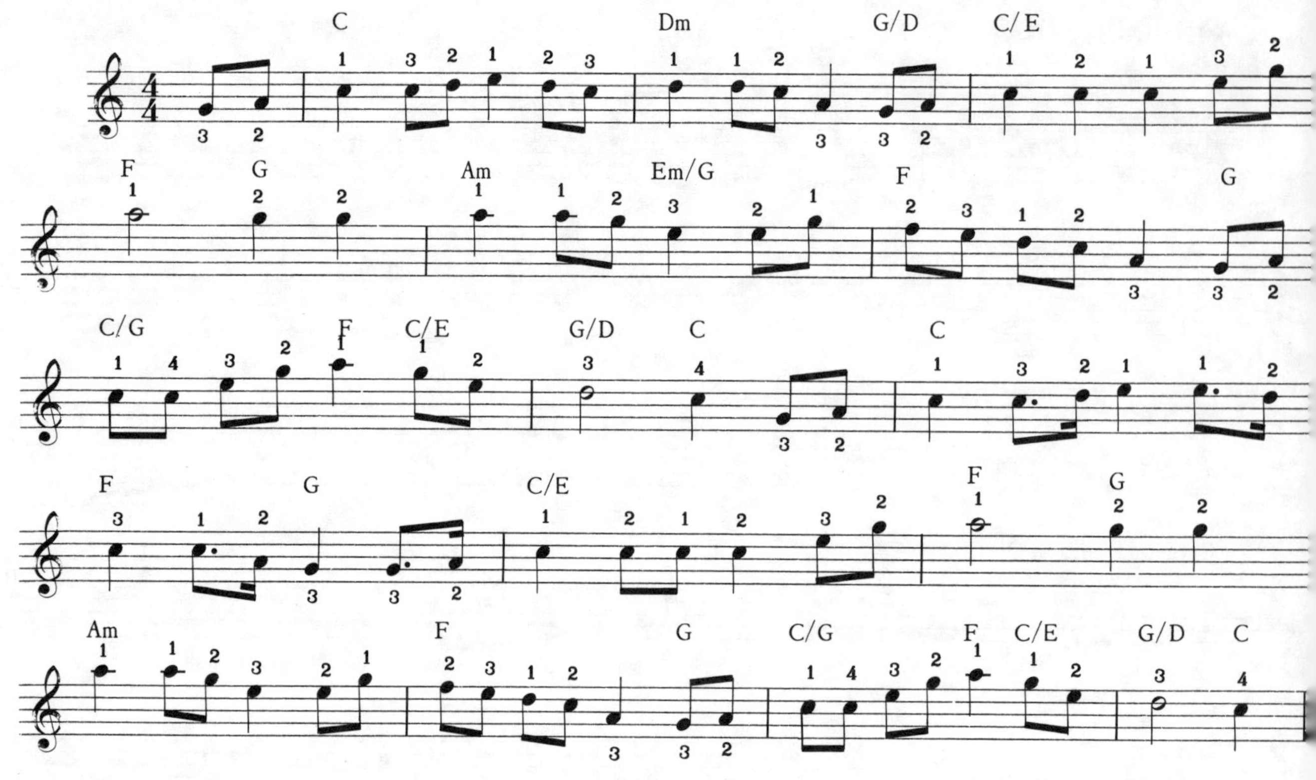

THE WIND FROM THE WEST

THE FANAID GROVE

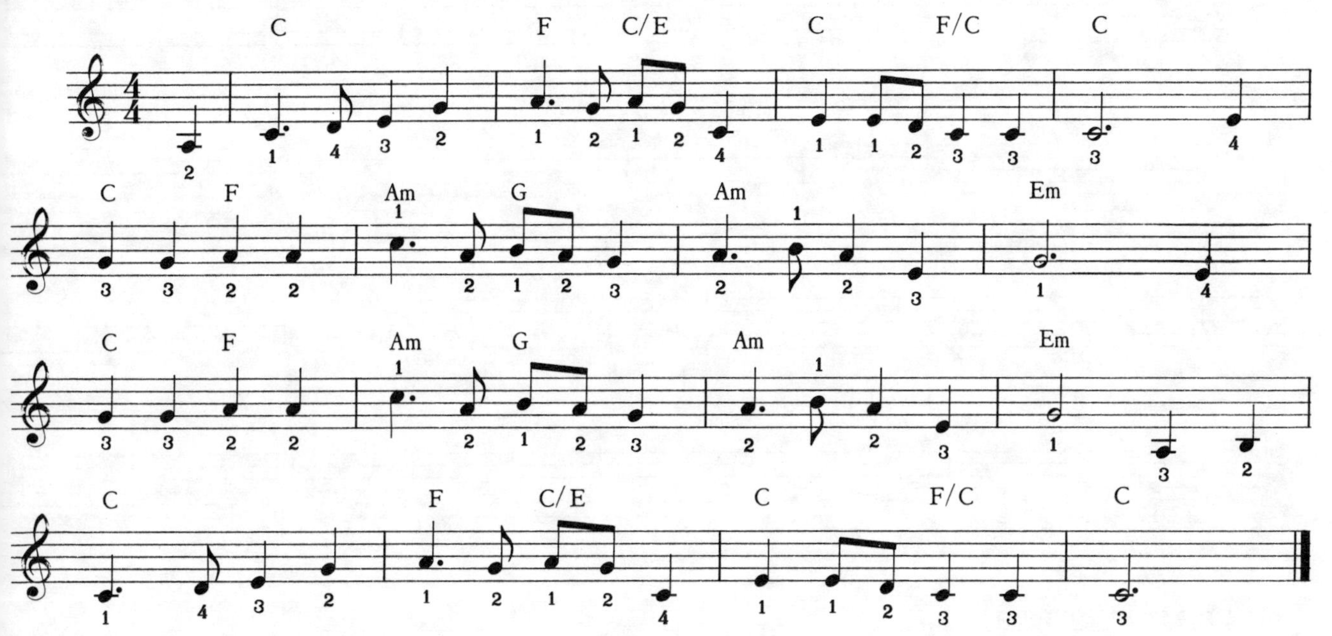

LEAVING OF LIVERPOOL

STEAL AWAY

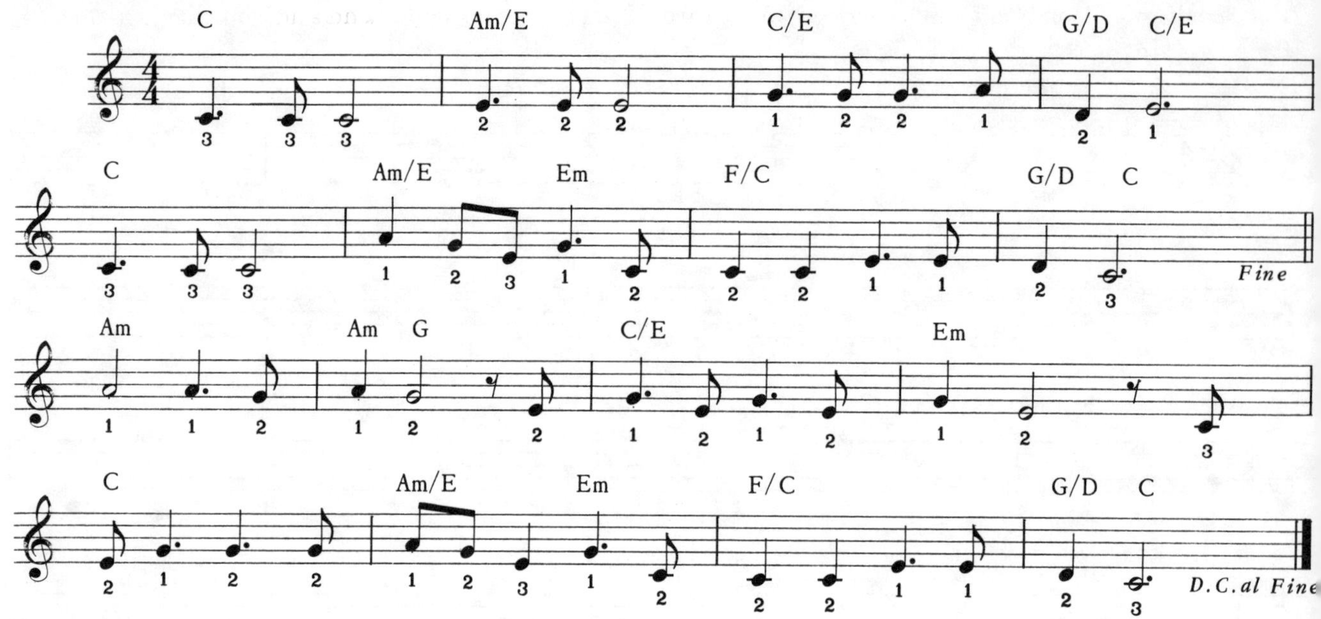

THE SIMPLE BIRTH

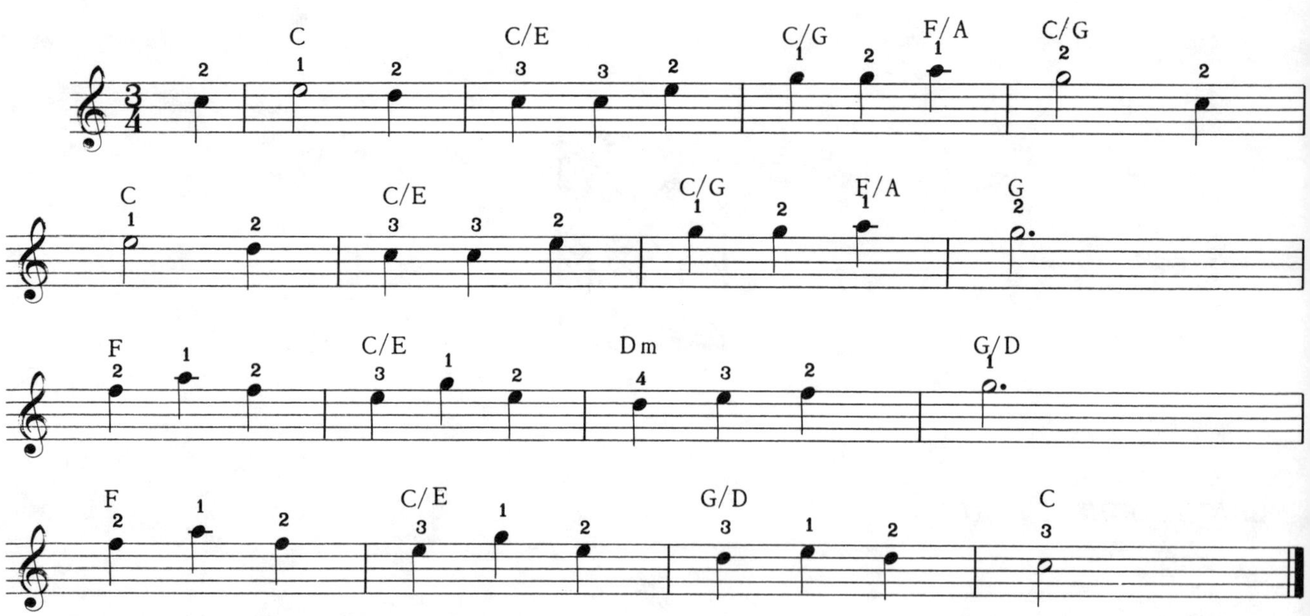

INVERSIONS ON FAST PIECES

Sometimes, pieces are so fast and the chords change so rapidly that it is hard to play all the chords in the root position; you have to move around too much. This is another instance where inversions come in very handy.

Here's an example. Try going back and forth between the root position chords C and F as fast as you can. It takes a bit of time to get from one to the other, and you usually have to look at the strings to make sure you're in the right place. Now, let's try an F chord in the second inversion (F/C). Put your fingers on C, F, and A. Now, to get the root position C chord, you just move the F and the A down one string to E and G.

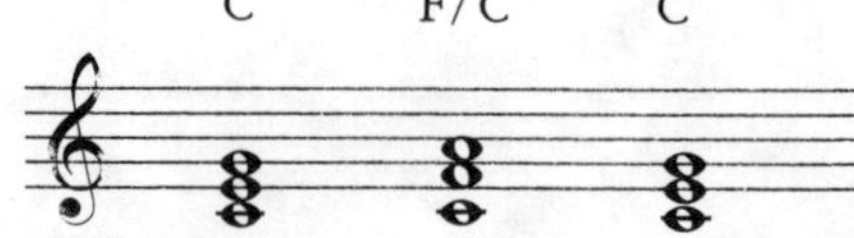

Once you get used to this, it is much quicker to move from C to F in this manner than to use both root positions. You don't have to move your third finger at all, just your 2nd and your thumb. Practice this until it feels comfortable.

There are 2 other choices you can use for moving between the C and F chords. Each time, whichever finger is on the C note will stay still, and the other two fingers will move.

Practice these, as well, until you get used to them. Be sure to practice all these exercises with your left hand, an octave lower than written.

Now let's try moving back and forth between root position C and G chords. As before, it is a long distance to move, it takes time, and usually you have to look. So, let's try using the inversions that make the movement as small as possible. Practice them until you can do them (with either hand) without having to think.

"Corn Rigs Are Bonnie" is a lively tune from Ireland and Scotland that has quite a few quick chord changes. Experiment with starting on different inversions for the first of the fast chords, and then try to find the closest inversions for the next chords. Keep experimenting until you find the ones that sound good to you and that keep you from having to move too far on the quick chords.

CORN RIGS

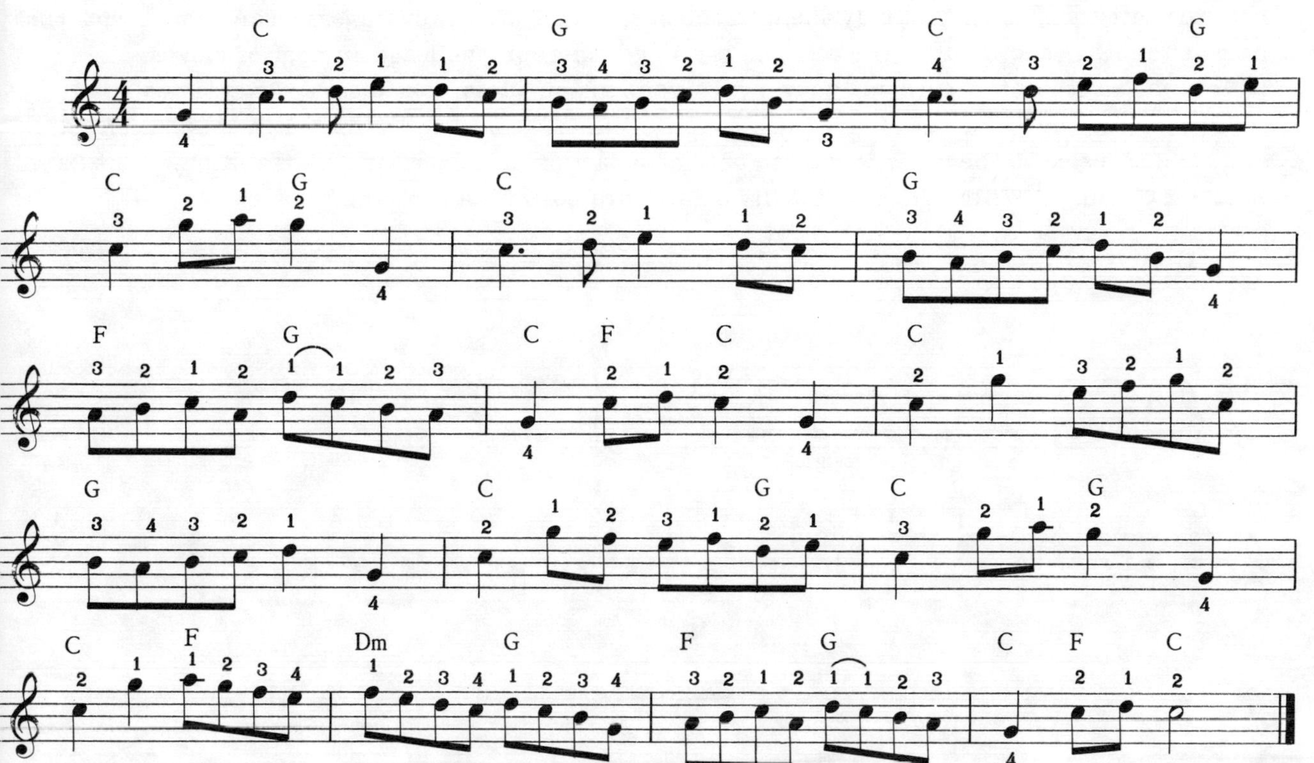

A good mental and finger exercise is to practice moving between various chords, trying to find the closest inversions. Most of the time you'll be able to keep at least one finger where it was on the previous chord. The only exception to this is when you move to a chord that is right next door in the alphabet to the one you were playing before. For example, when moving from F to G (since they are next to each other in the alphabet), or from F to E, you can just move all three fingers up or down one string, keeping the same inversion. All the rest of the time, you can keep at least one finger where it was.

We're now going to play the following random progression of chords. These chords are not in any logical order, I just "picked them out of the air". What I want you to do is play this progression of chords, trying to find *the closest inversion* each time. I've written out the actual chords that work when starting with a root position C chord. Play through these and notice that you hardly have to move your hand, just a few fingers. Once you get the hang of it, try not to read the notes, just figure them out yourself from the chord names. This exercise takes lots of concentration, but the results are well worth the time spent.

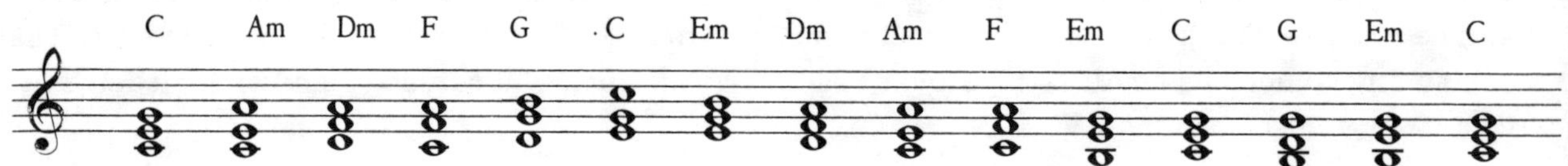

Now you're on your own. This time, play the same progression of chords, but start on a first inversion C chord and see where that takes you. Once again, be sure you're finding the CLOSEST inversion of the next chord. Check the appendix if you need some help.

C/E Am Dm F G C Em Dm Am F Em C G Em C

Start on a 2nd inversion C chord and play the progression again.

C/G Am Dm F G C Em Dm Am F Em C G Em C

You can make up your own random progressions of chords to practice like this. You don't even need to write them down, just play them on the harp. Start with your fingers on any chord, pick the name of another chord out of the air, and try to get there in the least number of moves.

Now you're ready to figure out your own inversions on these next pieces. Be creative!

"The Riddle" and "Barbara Allen" are popular folk songs which originated in the British Isles, and then traveled to the "new world" to become a part of the American folk tradition. "The Skye Boat Song" and "O Willy's Rare and Willy's Fair" are both from Scotland.

THE RIDDLE

BARBARA ALLEN

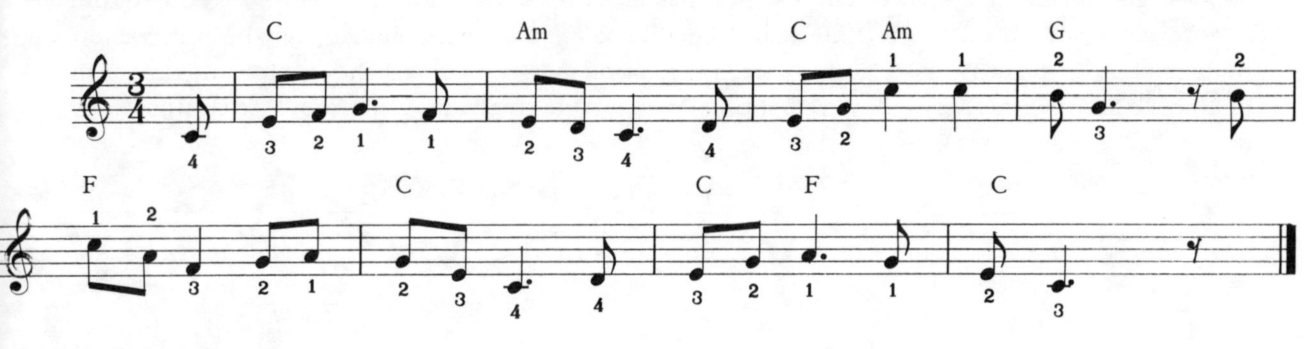

SKYE BOAT SONG

O WILLY'S RARE AND WILLY'S FAIR

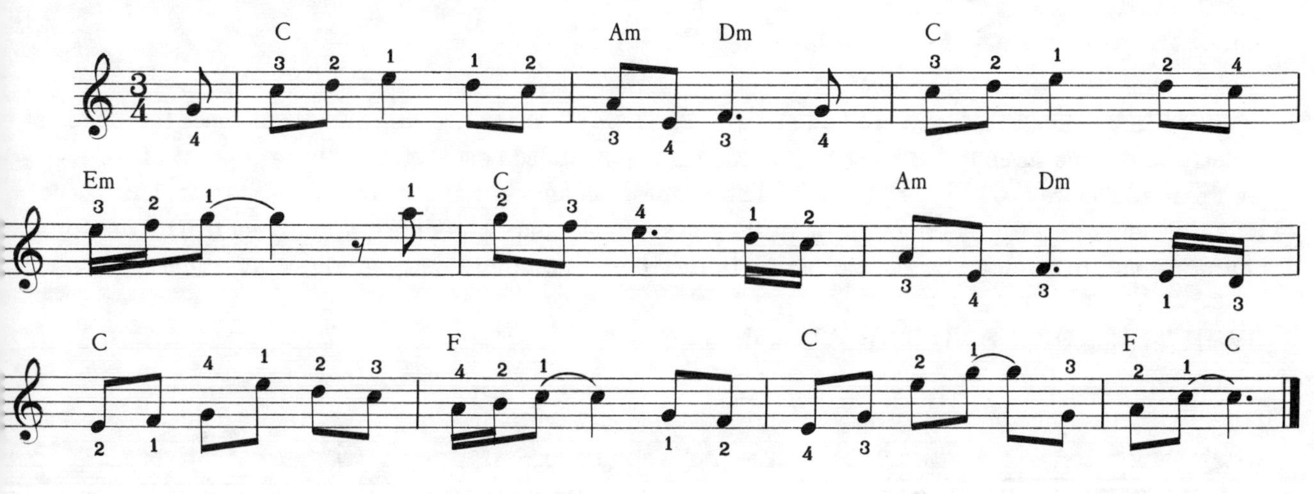

RUSSIAN HYMN

"Aura Lee" is an old folk song that was very popular during the American Civil War, but you may recognize it as the melody Elvis used for "Love Me Tender".

AURA LEE

Notice in the Irish tune "Over the Hills and Far Away", that three of the four phrases have almost exactly the same melody. However, I chose different chords each time, giving it a bit of variety. You can add more variety by changing the inversions as well. Another suggestion on this piece: when a measure only has one chord in it, you can still play the chord two times in the measure, changing the inversion the second time. Generally the second chord would come on beat "three".

OVER THE HILLS AND FAR AWAY

Chapter 5 - Four Note Chords

Up until now, we have been working with chords that have 3 notes. However, you can play as many of each of these three notes as you'd like. Since we use four fingers on each hand in playing the harp, it is often nice to play four note chords instead of three. The easiest way to do this is to add the octave. For example, to play a C chord, place your 4th, 3rd, and 2nd fingers on the C, E, and G (instead of using your 3rd, 2nd, and thumb as usual), and then add your thumb on the high C.

You can also do this with the inversions. Use fingers 4, 3, & 2 on the first three notes, and then add your thumb, an octave higher than your 4th finger.

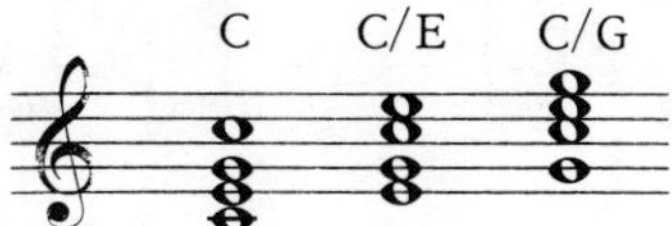

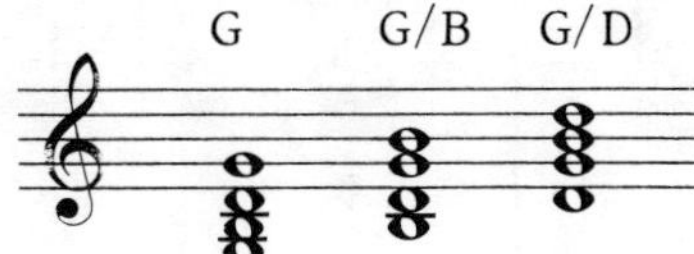

Practice playing 4-note chords with each hand (separately) until you feel comfortable with them. Be sure to practice all the inversions. Also, go back to the exercises on page 30 and try them with four note chords.

If you'd like, you can go back to some of the pieces you've been working on and add four note chords in places where you have enough room and you think they'll sound good.

Chapter 6 - Intervals And Half-Steps In Chords

To fully understand certain things about chords, intervals, and keys, we need to be acquainted with a piano keyboard. Many relationships can be seen more easily on a keyboard than on the harp.

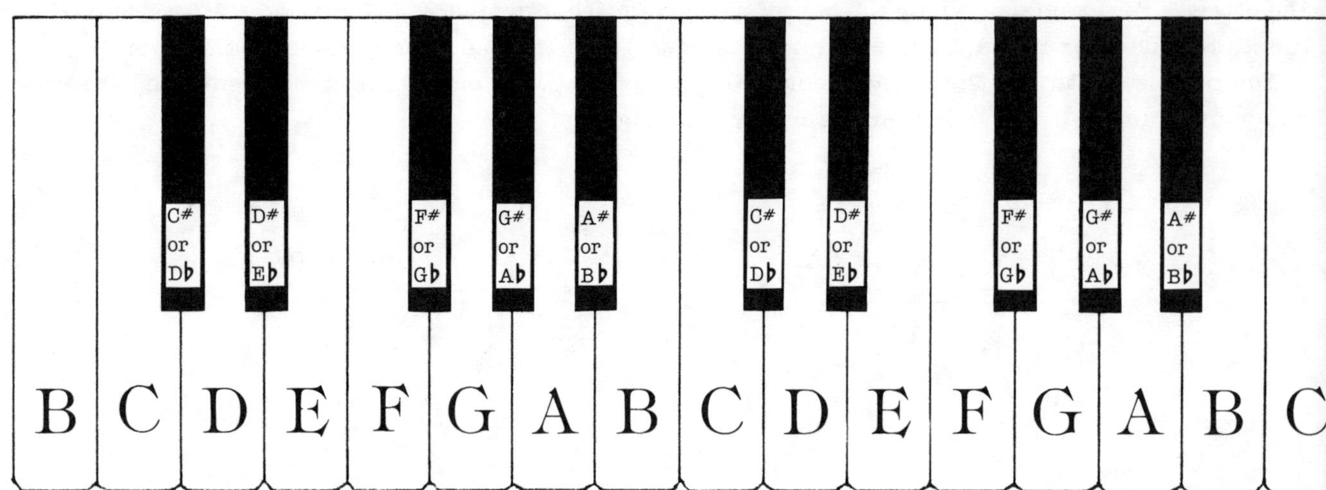

The distance between one key and the next adjacent key on the piano is called a "half-step". Even though F and G may look like they are adjacent, there is a black key between them, and therefore the half-steps would be from F to F# (F sharp), and another half-step from F# to G. Here are a few more examples: from G to G# is a half-step, from B♭ (B flat) to B is a half-step, from C to C# is a half-step, etc.

A half-step is not always between a black key and a white key. Sometimes there is only a half-step between two white keys. This happens if there is no black note between them. Between B and C is a half-step, as is the distance between E and F.

A whole-step, of course, is the same as two half-steps. For example, from F to G is two half-steps, or one whole-step; from C to D is a whole-step; from G# to A# is a whole-step; and so is from E to F#.

MAJOR CHORD INTERVALS

You can add half-steps and whole-steps together. For example, let's find out how many steps there are between the 3 notes of a root position C major chord. From C to E is 2 whole steps (C-C# = ½, C#-D = ½, giving a total of 1 step, D-D# = ½ totaling 1½, and D#-E = ½, for a grand total of 2 steps). Now count from E up to G, and you should get a total for that interval of 1½ steps. To summarize, a C major chord has 2 steps between the root and the third of the chord, and 1½ steps between the third and the fifth. Another way of saying this is that it has 2 steps on the "bottom" and 1½ steps on the "top".

Now count the number of steps between the notes of a root position G major chord. How many did you come up with? The correct answer is 2 steps on the "bottom" (between G and B) and 1½ steps on the "top" (from B to D). Notice that this is the same number of steps we found in the C major chord. Perhaps we're on to something! (If you got a different answer, go back and try again until you are sure you understand it.)

How many steps are there in a root position F major chord? Count them. The correct answer is 2 steps on the bottom (from F to A), and 1½ steps on the top (from A to C). This is the same pattern that we found on both the C major and the G major chord. From this we can deduce, my dear Watson, that every root position major chord in the universe has 2 steps between the root and the third (the bottom), and 1½ steps between the third and the fifth (the top). That's what makes the major chords sound like major chords.

Remember the intervals we learned earlier? We learned that in a C chord it is an interval of a 3rd between the C and E, and another interval of a 3rd between E and G. How come they both don't have the same number of half-steps in them? How come the 3rd between C and E has 2 steps, and the 3rd between E and G has only 1½ steps?

The answer to this question is that there are two different kinds of intervals that are called a 3rd. A "major 3rd" has 2 steps, and a "minor 3rd" has 1½ steps. So, we can say that all major chords have a "major 3rd" on the bottom, and a "minor 3rd" on the top. Try to remember that a major 3rd is a half-step LARGER than a minor 3rd.

Here's a quiz to help you learn the difference between major 3rds and minor 3rds. Below each interval, write whether it is a major 3rd, or a minor 3rd. When you're done, check you answers in the appendix.

INTERVALS OF A 3rd EXERCISE

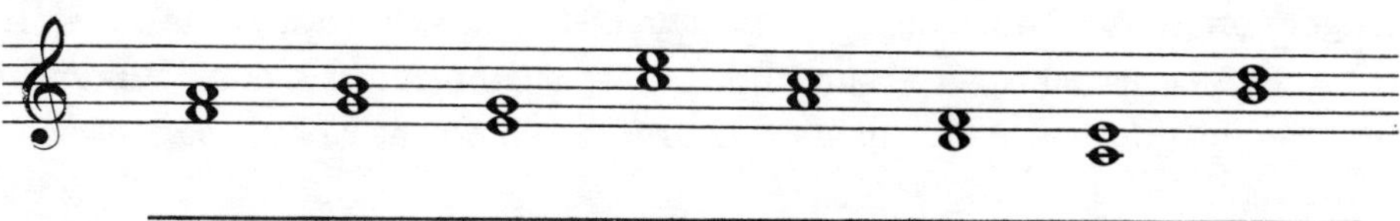

MINOR CHORD INTERVALS

Now that we've unraveled the mysteries of the major chords, let's look at the minor chords. How many steps are there in a root position D minor chord? Well, from D to F is 1½ (that's funny, in the major chord there were 2 steps on the bottom), and from F to A is 2 steps (hm, in the major chord there were only 1½ steps on the top). So, the Dm has 1½ steps on the bottom, and 2 steps on the top. Or, to word it another way, it has a minor 3rd on the bottom, and a major 3rd on the top.

How about an Am chord: A to C is 1½, C to E is 2. And now an Em chord: E to G is 1½, G to B is 2. Once again, minor 3rds on the bottom, and major 3rds on the top. Well, Watson, I think we've solved another case. All minor chords have a minor 3rd on the bottom, and a major 3rd on the top. This is just the opposite of the major chords.

An easy way to remember which is which, is to remember that major chords have a MAJOR 3rd on the bottom, and minor chords have a MINOR 3rd on the bottom.

Notice that in both the major and minor chords, the distance between the root and the 5th is the same: 3½ steps. For major chords, 2 steps on the bottom plus 1½ steps on the top = 3½ steps. For minor chords, 1½ steps on the bottom plus 2 steps on the top = 3½ steps. (Isn't mathematics amazing!). So, from this we can see that the root and the 5th are the same in major and minor chords; it is just the 3rd that is different. By the way, the interval from the root to the 5th in major or minor chords is called a "perfect 5th", which contains 3½ steps.

CHANGING MINOR CHORDS TO MAJOR CHORDS

Let's look at the D minor chord for a minute. What do you suppose we could do if we wanted to make it into a D MAJOR chord, instead? If your harp has sharping levers, put your fingers on a D minor chord (or try it on a piano). Like all other minor chords, it has 1½ steps on the bottom. Well, a major chord needs 2 steps on the bottom, so let's raise the 3rd of the chord by a half-step: with your sharping lever, raise the F to an F#, but keep the D and A where they were. What happened? We now have 2 steps on the bottom, and 1½ steps on the top. So, we now have a D MAJOR CHORD with the major 3rd on the bottom, and the minor 3rd on the top! Go back and forth between the D minor and D major chords (by engaging and disengaging your F# lever) and listen to the differences.

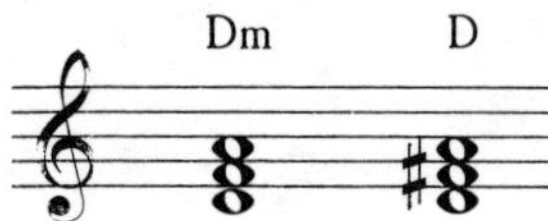

Now, put your fingers on an A minor chord. Raise the 3rd of the chord up a half-step (raise the C to C#). Once again, we have created an A Major chord, with 2 steps on the bottom and 1½ steps on top. Play both the A major and the A minor chords and listen to the changes.

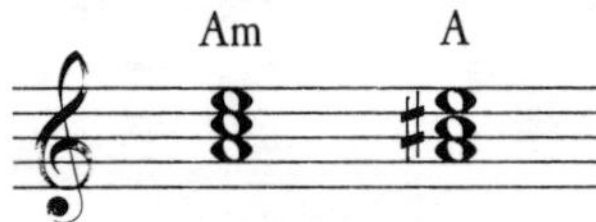

We have now discovered that the way to change a minor chord into a major chord is to raise the 3rd by a half-step. This will work every time. Conversely, to change a major chord into a minor chord, lower the 3rd by a half-step.

"NEUTRAL CHORDS"

When reading music in guitar books or other music books, you'll often find chords written that you do not easily have on your harp. For example, let's say we are playing a piece in the key of C (with no sharps or flats, as we've been playing so far), and the music suddenly asks for an A Major chord. Well, on our harps, the A chord is minor. So, what can we do? Well, we have several choices. Our first choice is to give up and go home . . . but we won't do that this time. Our second choice (if we have sharping levers on our harp) is to sharp the C when we see the A Major chord, and then natural it again for the C chord (or any other chord that needs a C natural). That can get quite complicated and tricky.

Our third choice is to play what I call a NEUTRAL chord. That is, leave out the middle note (the 3rd of the chord) and play only the root and the 5th. So, for an A chord, you'd just play the A and the E, and leave out the C. That way, it doesn't sound either major or minor; it just sounds "neutral".

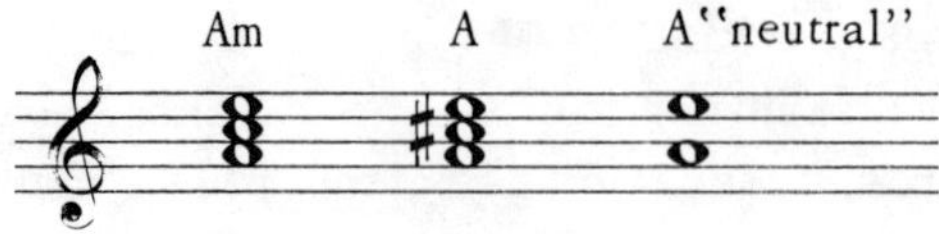

We'll be trying "neutral chords" on some pieces later in this book.

Chapter 7 Diminished And Augmented Chords

There are several other types of chords besides major and minor. Have you wondered why we have not used any B chords in this book? Play a B chord (B, D, F) on your harp.

Can you hear that it sounds different from the chords we've played before? It certainly doesn't sound major, but it doesn't really sound minor, either. It is called a diminished chord. It is made up of two *minor* 3rds: 1½ steps on the bottom, and 1½ steps on the top. There is no major 3rd as there is in either a major or minor chord. The notation for a diminished chord is either "dim" or a superscript ° like this: b^{dim} or b°.

Another interesting chord is an augmented chord. It is made up of two *major* 3rds, each containing 2 steps. This chord does not fall naturally on your harp, but an example would be C augmented: C, E, G#. The notation for an augmented chord is either "aug" or a "+" sign: C^{aug} or C^{+}.

Diminished and augmented chords are rarely used in folk music, but are more common in jazz and modern music.

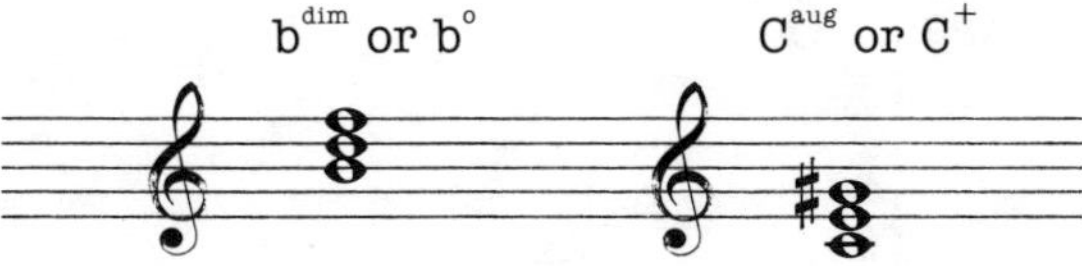

Chapter 8 - Major Keys

A key signature is the group of sharps or flats written at the beginning of a piece of music. It appears right after the clef sign and right before the time signature. This key signature tells you what notes will be sharp or flat throughout the entire piece. This also tells you what key the piece is in. So far, we haven't really noticed key signatures in this book, because the pieces have not had any sharps or flats. Therefore, the key signature was blank.

Here are some examples of what key signatures look like:

The major key we have been working with is the key of C major, which has no sharps or flats. One of the easiest ways to tell what notes are in a certain major key is to try to play a "do re mi" scale, starting on the note that is the name of the key. For example, start on C and play an ascending scale (C, D, E, F, G, A, B, C). If your harp is tuned with no sharps or flats, it should sound like a regular "do re mi" scale. This tells you that you are tuned to the key of C major, and that the key of C major has no sharps or flats.

Now, try the same thing starting on G. As you play this ascending scale, you'll notice that it sounds fine until you get to the F note, which doesn't sound right. This is because the key of G has an F# in it. Sharp the F and then try the G scale again: now it should sound right. From this we can discover that the key of G has one sharp: F#.

Let's try the same thing starting on D. When we play this ascending scale, we discover that in order to get the proper "do re mi" scale, we have to sharp both the F and the C. So, the key of D has two sharps: F# and C#.

Remember, back in the chapters about major and minor chords, we discovered that all major chords had the same pattern of half-steps in them? Well, there is also a common half-step relationship in all major scales. The major scale ("do re mi" scale), always has half-steps between the 3rd and the 4th notes, and between the 7th and the 8th notes. All of the other scale notes have a whole step between them. In these examples, the half-steps are indicated by the "‿".

By using this pattern of whole-steps and half-steps, we can form major scales starting on other notes, and thus discover what sharps are in those keys.

KEY	NO. OF SHARPS	NAMES OF SHARPS						
C	0							
G	1	F						
D	2	F	C					
A	3	F	C	G				
E	4	F	C	G	D			
B	5	F	C	G	D	A		
F#	6	F	C	G	D	A	E	
C#	7	F	C	G	D	A	E	B

The sharps always come in the same order. The first is always F#, the second C#, the next G#, etc. As you add a sharp to the key signature, you keep the sharps that were there before. For example, the key of A has 3 sharps: F#, C#, and G#. The key of E has 4 sharps: the same 3 plus D#.

There are several mnemonic devices you can use to help you remember what order the sharps come in. In these sentences the first letter of each word stands for the name of the sharp. You can use any of these sentences, or make up your own. "Fat Cats Get Drunk At Every Bar"; or "Fast Cars Go Driving Around Every Block"; or "Funny Cows Go Dancing And Eat Beans".

Notice that the order the sharps come in are an interval of a perfect 5th apart. (Remember that a perfect 5th contains 3½ steps.) From F# to C# is a 5th, from C# to G# is a 5th, etc. The names of the keys are also a perfect 5th apart: the first key is C, then the next key is G (up a 5th), then D, etc.

If you see a key signature with sharps at the beginning of a piece of music, and you want to figure out what key it is, there is a simple way of remembering. Look at the *LAST* sharp in the key signature and go up a half-step; that will be the name of the key. For example, if there is only one sharp in the key signature, that sharp will be F#; go up a half-step from F#, and that tells you that the key is G. For 2 sharps, the last sharp is C#; go up a half-step, and the key is D.

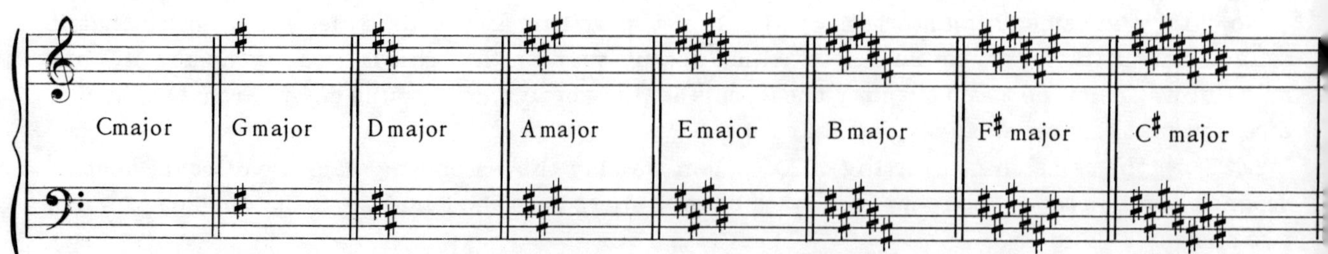

If you have your folk harp tuned to the key of C, the flat keys are a bit harder to hear, since you on't have them on your harp. (This, of course, is not a problem on a pedal harp.) However, you can gure them out in the same way; making a "do re mi" scale following our same series of whole and alf-steps. If you play an ascending scale starting on F, the B note sounds funny. That is because it hould be a B♭. The key of F has one flat: B♭.

By the way, if you want to play tunes in flat keys on your folk harp, you can tune your strings own to the flats *WHEN YOU TUNE THEM.* For example, to play in the key of F, tune your B strings B♭ when you tune your harp. Since engaging your sharping lever will raise the pitch of the string a half-step, when you want to go back to playing in the key of C, use your sharping levers on our B strings. This will raise the pitch by a half-step from B♭ back to B natural. Likewise, to play the key of E♭, you would tune all of the B, E, and A strings on your harps to *FLATS* when you ne your harp; then engage the levers on those strings to return to the key of C.

Here are the flat keys:

KEY	NO. OF FLATS	NAMES OF FLATS						
C	0							
F	1	B						
B♭	2	B	E					
E♭	3	B	E	A				
A♭	4	B	E	A	D			
D♭	5	B	E	A	D	G		
G♭	6	B	E	A	D	G	C	
C♭	7	B	E	A	D	G	C	F

Notice that the flats go in the opposite order from the sharps. They go down a 5th from the first at to the next, instead of up a 5th as the sharps did. The keys also go down a 5th from one to the ext.

There are two ways to remember which order the flats come in. The first four flats spell the word ead". Or, here's a sentence using all seven flats: "By Evening, Arctic Dogs Get Cold Feet".

If you have a key signature with flats in it, the name of the key will be the name of the NEXT-TO-HE-LAST FLAT. For example, if you have 4 flats (B♭, E♭, A♭, D♭) the next-to-the-last flat is A♭, which the name of the key. You'll just have to memorize that 1 flat is the key of F, because since there is ly one flat, there can't be a "next-to-the-last flat".

C major | F major | B♭ major | E♭ major | A♭ major | D♭ major | G♭ major | C♭ major

EXERCISE

Figure out which MAJOR KEYS the key signatures indicate.
Check your answers in the appendix.

Chapter 9 - Minor Keys

With our harps tuned with no sharps or flats, we are in the key of C major, but we could also be i the key of A minor, instead. This is because each major key has a "relative minor key", which ha the same number of sharps or flats. The key signature for the keys of C major and A minor are th same (no sharps or flats), and so they are called "relative keys". The way you can tell which key piece is in is by its sound and the chords that are most often used. Most of the pieces that you playe in the chapter on minor chords were actually in the key of A minor, instead of the key of C. The started and ended on A minor chords, and the majority of the chords in the pieces were min chords.

If you look at a key signature and figure out what major key it represents, just go down a min 3rd from the name of that major key to get the name of the relative minor key. For example: n sharps or flats is the key of C major; go down a minor 3rd from C and you come up with "A", which the name of the relative minor key (A minor).

Let's try another example. The major key that has one sharp is the key of G major. What is an in terval of a minor 3rd down from G? The correct answer is E. Therefore, the relative minor key to major is E minor. They both have one sharp in the key signature.

Here's a chart of the major keys and their relative minor keys.

CHART OF SHARPS

	MAJOR KEY	MINOR KEY
0	C	Am
1	G	Em
2	D	Bm
3	A	F#m
4	E	C#m
5	B	G#m
6	F#	D#m
7	C#	A#m

CHART OF FLATS

	MAJOR KEY	MINOR KEY
0	C	Am
1	F	Dm
2	B♭	Gm
3	E♭	Cm
4	A♭	Fm
5	D♭	B♭ m
6	G♭	E♭ m
7	C♭	A♭ m

Go back to the exercise at the top of this page, and figure out which MINOR KEYS the k signatures indicate. Check your answers in the appendix.

Chapter 10 - Key Of G Major

Now that we know something about various keys, let's try some pieces in the key of G major. As you remember, the key of G has one sharp: F#. So, to start with, you'll need to sharp all the F's on your harp.

Because our F's are now F#s, any chord that contains an F note will sound different than it did before. For example, in the key of C, our D chord was D minor (D, F, A). Now, in the key of G, our D chord will be MAJOR (D, F#, A). Also, our B diminished chord that we never used in the key of C, now becomes a useful B minor (B, D, F#). And our F chord that we used so much in the key of C becomes F# diminished (F#, A, C). All the other chords will be the same as they were in the key of C.

So now, with all our F's sharped, we're ready to try some pieces in the key of G. Figure out your own inversions for the chords and write them in, so you won't forget them.

These pieces are all from the British Isles. "The Spotted Cow" is English, "Megan's Fair Daughter" is Welsh, and the remainder are from Ireland.

THE SPOTTED COW

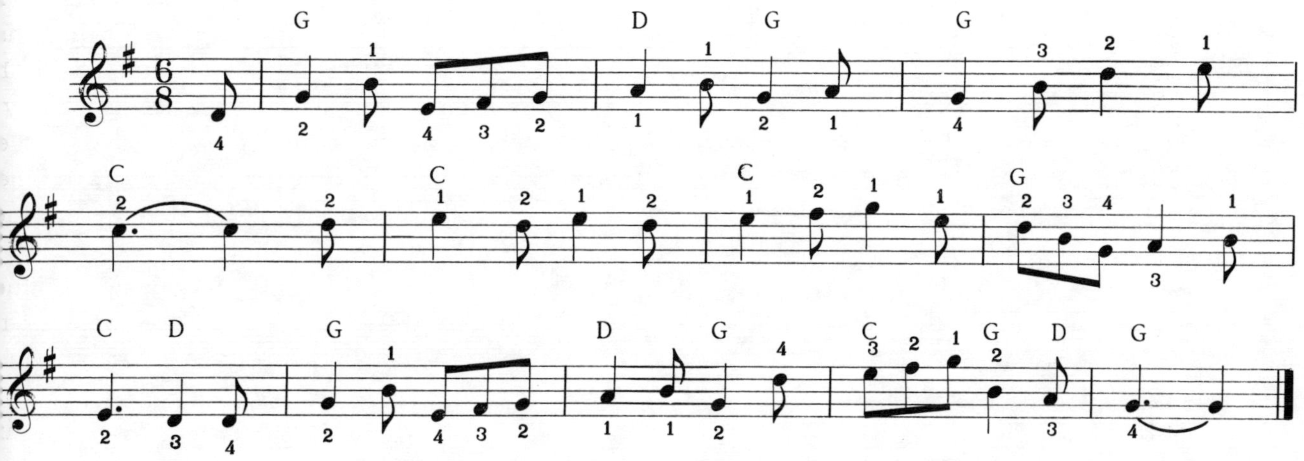

LIMERICK IS BEAUTIFUL

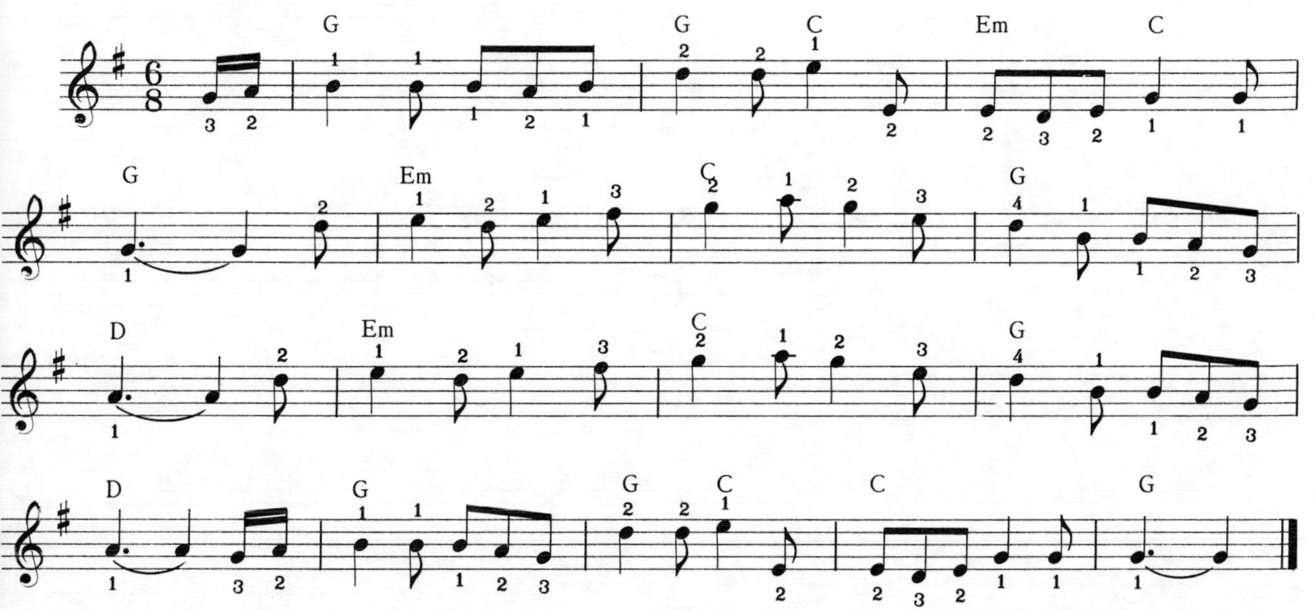

MEGAN'S FAIR DAUGHTER
G C Am D
G C C D G
G C Am D
G C C D G
G D Em D
G D Em D
G C Am D
G C C D G
I'M A POOR STRANGER
G G C G
C G Em Bm
C G Em D
Em G C G

BELIEVE ME IF ALL THOSE ENDEARING YOUNG CHARMS

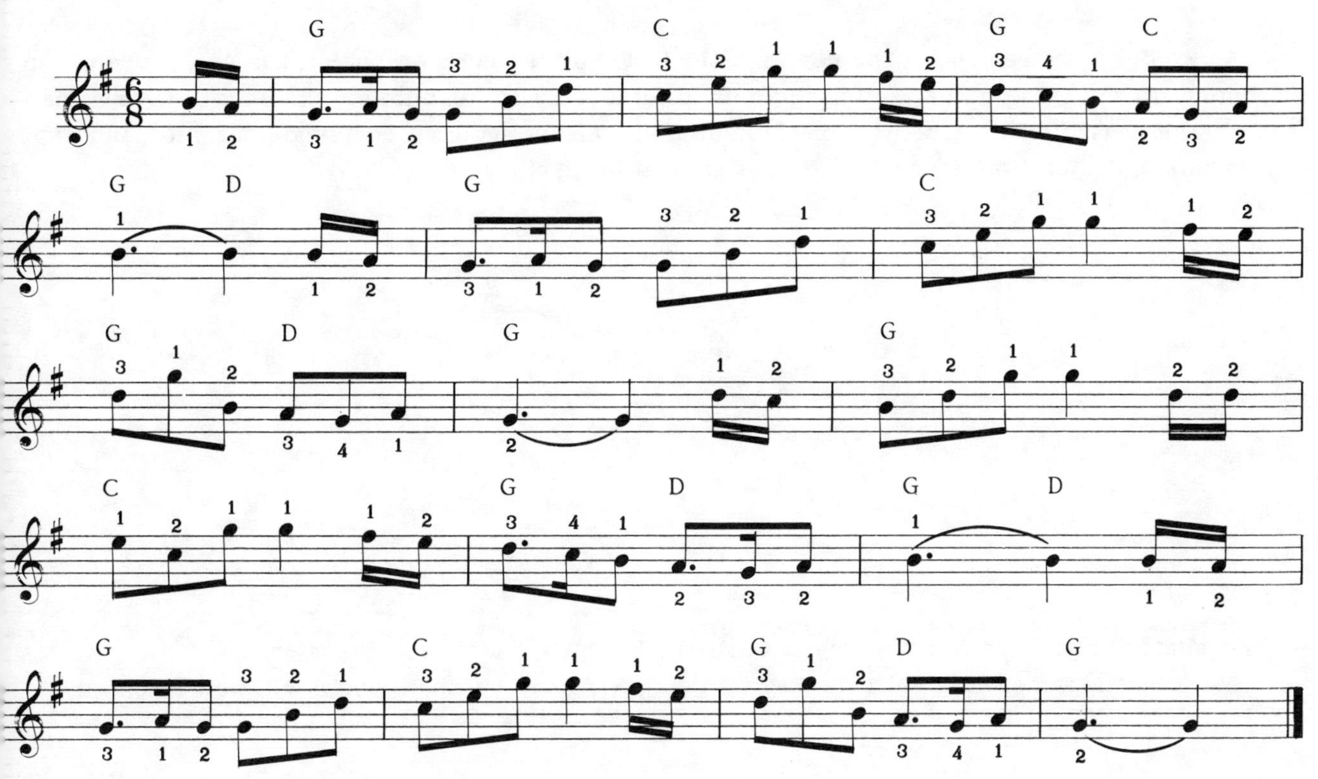

DOWN BY THE SALLEY GARDENS

Chapter 11 - Chord Relationships In Keys

As we discussed earlier, in the key of C, the C, F, and G chords are major; the Am, Dm, and Em chords are minor; and the B dim chord is diminished. If we number the chords with roman numerals as is often done (using capital roman numerals for major chords, small for minor, and with a superscript ° for diminished) we will get the following chart.

KEY	I	ii	iii	IV	V	vi	vii°
C	C	Dm	Em	F	G	Am	B°

This chart shows us that in the key of C, the I, IV, and V chords are all major.

Let's try the same thing with the key of G major. Of course, the G chord will now be chord I.

KEY	I	ii	iii	IV	V	vi	vii°
G	G	Am	Bm	C	D	Em	F#°

By comparing these two charts, we realize one more amazing rule of the universe: in any major key, the I, IV, and V chords are ALWAYS major. This, of course, means that the ii, iii and vi chords will always be minor, and the vii chord will be diminished.

You have that extreme look of doubt on your face. Well, try some more major keys and you will discover that it is, in fact, true.

MAJOR KEYS CHART

KEY	I	ii	iii	IV	V	vi	vii°
C	C	Dm	Em	F	G	Am	B°
D	D	Em	F#m	G	A	Bm	C#°
E♭	E♭	Fm	Gm	A♭	B♭	Cm	D°
F	F	Gm	Am	B♭	C	Dm	E°
G	G	Am	Bm	C	D	Em	F#°
A	A	Bm	C#m	D	E	F#m	G#°
B♭	B♭	Cm	Dm	E♭	F	Gm	A°

MINOR KEYS

In the minor keys, the configuration is a bit different, but the principle is the same. In the minor keys the i, iv and v chords are now MINOR. the III, VI and VII are major, and the ii is diminished. Here's a chart of some of the minor keys.

MINOR KEYS CHART

KEY	i	ii°	III	iv	v	VI	VII
Am	Am	B°	C	Dm	Em	F	G
Bm	Bm	C#°	D	Em	F#m	G	A
Cm	Cm	D°	E♭	Fm	Gm	A♭	B♭
Dm	Dm	E°	F	Gm	Am	B♭	C
Em	Em	F#°	G	Am	Bm	C	D
F#m	F#m	G#°	A	Bm	C#m	D	E
Gm	Gm	A°	B♭	Cm	Dm	E♭	F

So, the most important thing to remember is that whatever key you are in, the most useful and common chords will be "1", "4", and "5". That is, in the major keys, the major chords are I, IV and V, and in the minor keys, the minor chords are i, iv, and v, and those are the ones you'll use the most.

QUIZ

1. In the key of C
   the three major chords are: __________
   the three minor chords are: __________
   the diminished chord is: __________

2. In the key of G
   the three major chords are: __________
   the three minor chords are: __________
   the diminished chord is: __________

3. In the key of A
   the three major chords are: __________
   the three minor chords are: __________
   the diminished chord is: __________

4. In the key of D
   the three major chords are: __________
   the three minor chords are: __________
   the diminished chord is: __________

5. In the key of F
   the three major chords are: __________
   the three minor chords are: __________
   the diminished chord is: __________

6. In the key of B♭
   the three major chords are: __________
   the three minor chords are: __________
   the diminished chord is: __________

Chapter 12 - Additional Chords

SEVENTH CHORDS

As we discussed earlier, every chord is made up of a root note, a 3rd, and a 5th. However, sometimes chords have additional notes.

Be sure your harp is tuned back into the key of C. Put three fingers on a G chord, but don't use your thumb: put your 4th finger on G, your 3rd on B, and your 2nd on D. Now, put your thumb on F. Yes, I said F, not G. This is called a G7 chord. This is because we started with G, and added an interval of a 7th above the G. So now we have a root, a 3rd, a 5th and a 7th. This is a G7 chord. Notice that in this root position of a 7th chord, you skip one string between all four fingers. Practice playing G7 chords up and down your harp.

G7

There are two kinds of 7th chords that can be made from major chords. Play the G7 chord again. Now play a C7 chord (C, E, G, B).

Can you hear that they sound different? Play the two of them again, and listen to the 7ths. They don't sound the same because the intervals of the 7ths in the two chords have a different number of half-steps. From G to F in the G7 chord is 5 steps; from C to B in the C7 chord is 5½ steps.

The 7th in the C7 chord is called a "major 7th". One way to think of a major 7th is to remember that it is as big as it can possibly be. If it was a half-step bigger, it would be an octave, instead of a 7th. It is written as "major 7" or "maj 7". Notice that the word "major" refers to the kind of 7th, not the kind of chord. And so, the proper name for this C7 chord is: C major 7.

The 7th in the G7 chord has several names. Sometimes it is called a "dominant 7th", or a "flatted 7th". However, it is usually just called a G7. And so if you see a chord that just has "7" written after it (with no "major"), then it should be this type of 7th. In this chord, the 7th is a full-step away from the octave (i.e. in the G7 chord, the F is a full step lower than the octave G). This is the most common type of 7th chord in folk music, and generally comes on the V chord. That is, if you're in the key of C, your most common 7th chord will be a G7; if you're in the key of G, it will be a D7, etc.

You can make 7th chords out of minor chords, too. Try playing an Am7 chord (A, C, E, G); a Dm7 (D, F, A, C); and an Em7 (E, G, B, D).

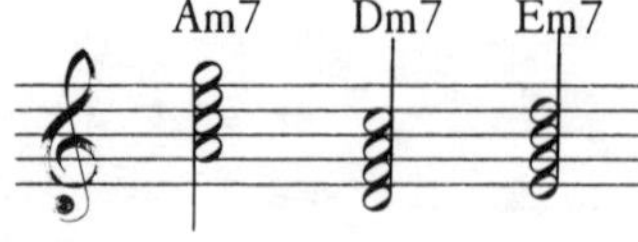

INVERSIONS OF 7TH CHORDS

Seventh chords can be inverted, just like "regular" chords. The root position of a G7 chord is, of course, G, B, D, F; the first inversion is B, D, F, G; the second inversion is D, F, G, B; and the third inversion is F, G, B, D. Notice that there are 3 inversions, since there are 4 different notes. Play these inversions until they feel comfortable. Try them on other 7th chords as well.

Experiment with using different inversions of the 7th chords in the American Shaker hymn, "Simple Gifts". You'll find that some inversions definitely sound better than others in each instance.

SIMPLE GIFTS

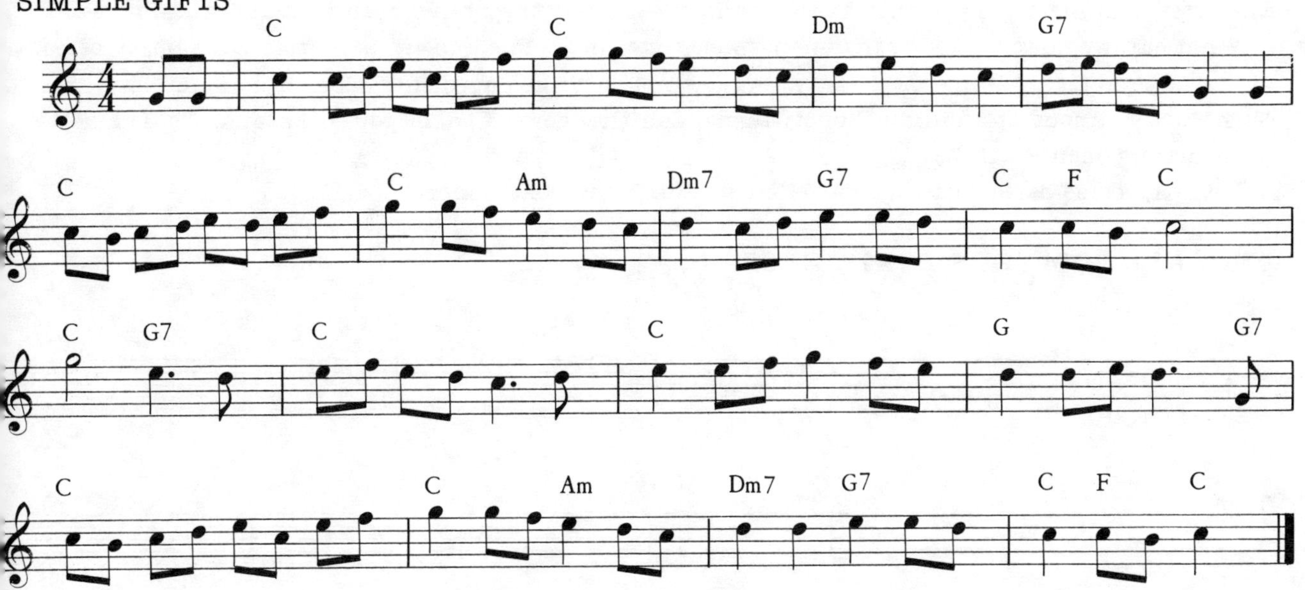

NINTH CHORDS

Starting with a dominant 7th chord, you can continue adding notes on top, skipping a string each time, to form 9th chords, 11th chords, and 13th chords. A 13th is as big as we go, because it uses all seven notes on your harp. For example, a G13 would be G, B, D, F, A, C, E; and that's all the notes you have available.

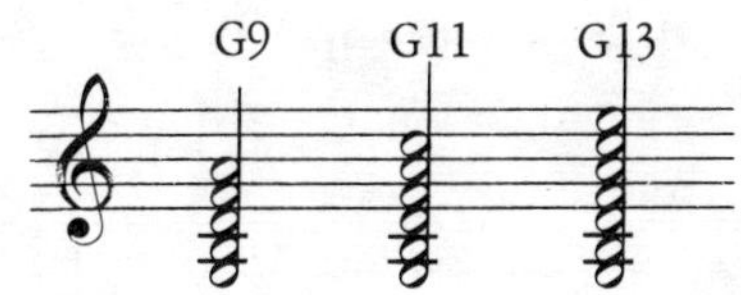

However, an important thing to remember when you see these chords asked for in music, is that you don't have to play all the notes. When playing a 13th chord, for example, you can leave out the 9th and the 11th.

Sometimes the melody will supply the added note. For example, suppose the melody note is an "A", and the music asks for a G9 chord. All you need to play in the left hand is a regular G chord, and the melody will supply the 9th (the "A").

Using 7th, 9th, 11th, and 13th chords help add variety to your arrangements. Experiment with them and get used to how they sound.

A lot of "modern", pop, and jazz music uses these and other more complex chords, and they are vital to the sound of the music. However, as you probably have discovered, non-pedal harps have a lot of trouble playing much of this music, because of our lack of readily available sharps and flats. If you are a pedal harpist and are interested in pop or jazz, you will need to refer to other theory books that contain more in-depth study of these "complex" chords.

SIXTH CHORDS

Another type of chord that you may run across is a 6th. A G6 would be G, B, D, E, with E being an interval of a 6th above G. Notice that this is the same as the first inversion of an Em7 chord. You could call this chord either a G6 or an Em7, depending on the context.

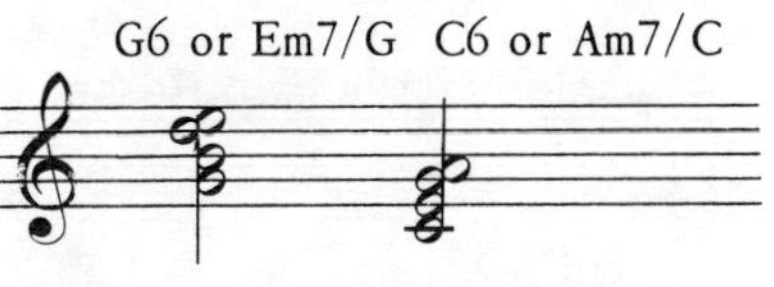

Chapter 13 - Patterns

What is arranging? Basically it is taking a melody and adding chords. If you've played the pieces so far in this book, you have actually been making arrangements. Granted, they may not have been the most exciting arrangements known to mankind, but they have been arrangements.

What can we do to make arrangements more exciting? The answer is patterns; a variety of patterns. By "patterns" I mean re-arranging the notes of the chord in various orders and rhythms. There are "billions and billions" of patterns; and the more of them you know and use, the better your arrangements will be.

Let's try some basic patterns on "Michael Row Your Boat Ashore".

MICHAEL ROW YOUR BOAT ASHORE

The pattern we've been using throughout this book so far is this: "play all the notes of the chord with your left hand on the first beat of each measure". Actually, you could argue that we have used several patterns, since sometimes we played the chord in the root position, and sometimes in an inversion.

Another common pattern is to play one note of the chord on each beat. For example, since this piece is in 4/4 time, you could play a C chord like this:

Practice "Michael Row Your Boat Ashore" using this pattern in your left hand (changing chords, of course, when indicated). The first few measures will be played like this:

Another pattern would be:

This pattern is a bit easier than the first pattern, because you don't play anything on the 4th beat: it gives you a "free" beat which allows you time to get to the next chord. You don't have to be quite as speedy. Try "Michael" using this pattern. The first few measures will be like this:

This next pattern is similar to the first pattern, except that we've changed the rhythm. Once again, it has a "free" 4th beat to give you time to change chords:

You don't always just have to go *UP* in a pattern; sometimes you can go *DOWN*, instead. Also, you can leave out some of the notes in the chord. This next pattern goes both up and down, and leaves out the 3rd of the chord.

Try "Michael" once again, using this pattern. It would start like this:

Sometimes you can even leave out the first beat!

You can play as many chords in each measure as you want.

These are just a few of the many, many patterns you could use on this piece, or any piece in 4/4 time.

Now, let's try a piece in 3/4 time: "Silent Night".

SILENT NIGHT

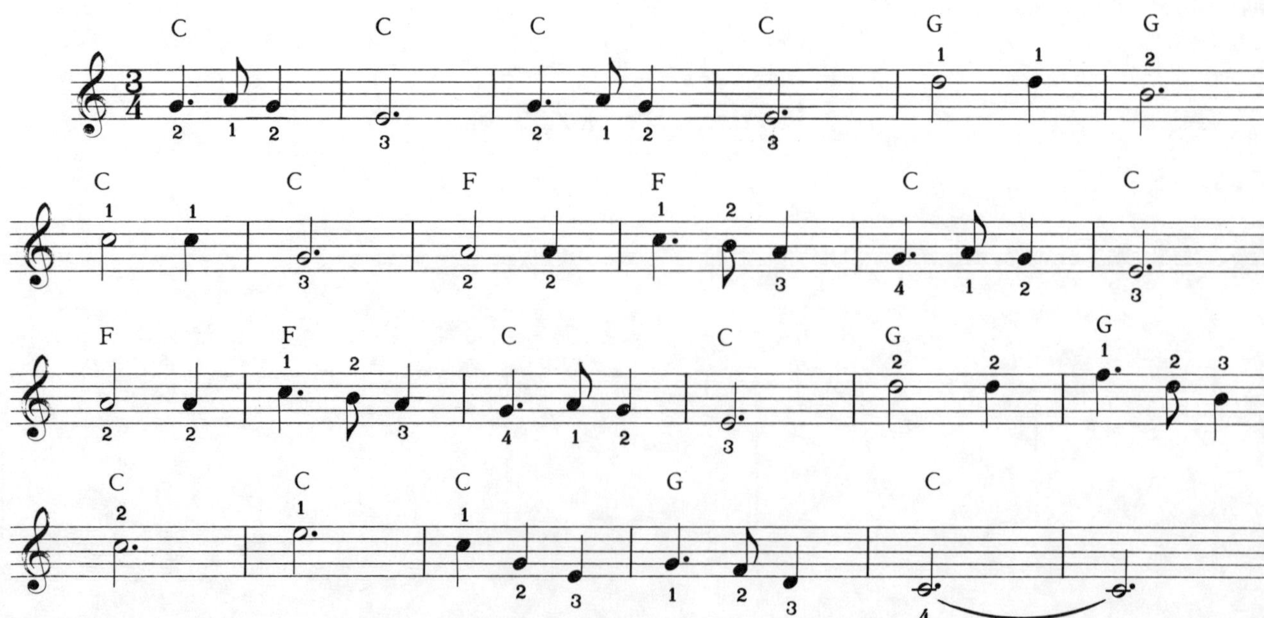

We'll start with some patterns that are variations of the ones we used in 4/4 time in "Michael Row Your Boat Ashore". We'll have to alter the patterns a bit to fit them into 3/4 time, but they'll follow many of the same principles.

Play "Silent Night" using the first of these patterns, and then play it all the way through again using the second pattern, and then the third, etc. Really LISTEN to what you are playing. Pay attention to which measures you think sound the best with each pattern.

VARIETY

Once you get used to adding various patterns in your left hand, it is time to be more creative. Playing a piece all the way through using only one pattern, as we have been doing, usually sounds pretty boring. Variety, as they say, is the spice of arranging.

Do you remember which patterns you liked best in each individual measure of "Silent Night"? Play it again, and this time, use several different patterns throughout the piece, and see how it makes your arrangement more interesting.

These are just a few of the patterns that you can use in your arrangements. Look at the following charts to get an idea of just SOME of the possible patterns you can use. Notice that in these charts, I just used the C chord, and only in the root position. I did this for clarity, so that the differences in the patterns would be easier to see. Of course, you can use them on any chord, and most of them work well in various inversions. I have included some blank staves for you to add your own patterns.

ACCOMPANIMENT PATTERNS IN 4/4 TIME

ACCOMPANIMENT PATTERNS IN 3/4 TIME

ACCOMPANIMENT PATTERNS IN 6/8 TIME

Sometimes, one chord will last for more than one measure. For example, in "Silent Night", most of the chords last for 2 measures before they change to another chord. In these instances, you can use accompaniment patterns that are two measures long. Try this next pattern on "Silent Night". Then make up other 2-measure patterns to use in this piece to help it flow better.

We often have the opposite problem in a piece: that is, the chords change in the MIDDLE of the measure, so we can only use half of the patterns we have figured out. In these instances, we have to be creative. Sometimes you can just play half of a pattern for each chord, and that will work fine. Or perhaps, speed up the notes in the pattern so they'll fit. Or even just play one or two notes of the chord, and that will sound fine. You just have to try different notes and rhythms to see what will sound the best in each circumstance. Try playing "Swing Low, Sweet Chariot", and experiment with which patterns (and which parts of patterns) work best in the measures where the chords change.

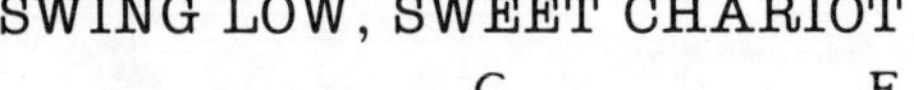

SWING LOW, SWEET CHARIOT

Pick a piece in this book that you like, and try playing it all the way through using only one pattern. Then play it using a different pattern; and then another, listening to the differences the various patterns make. Sometimes you may like the way one pattern sounds, except for certain measures; or a pattern may sound good in one part of a piece, but not in another. Really *LISTEN* to what you are playing, because these patterns will form the basis of your future arranging. Then, make an arrangement using a variety of the patterns that you liked in specific places in the piece. An easy way to start is to change your pattern on the last measure of every line or phrase, or use one set of patterns on the "chorus" and a different set on the "verse".

Practice LOTS OF PIECES using LOTS OF DIFFERENT PATTERNS, until you feel comfortable with them. Also, feel free to make up your own patterns or find new ones in other written music. As I said, the ones on these charts are not the only ones available.

Become very familiar with as many patterns as you can. I cannot over-stress the importance of knowing lots of patterns. Of course you'll have your favorites and "old stand-bys", but don't get stuck in a rut. I'm sure we've all heard "musicians" who make their own arrangements, and all of their songs sound alike. "When you've heard one, you've heard 'em all", so to speak. In many cases, this is because they only use 2 or 3 patterns (or sometimes only 1!), and so their arrangements all sound the same.

By knowing (and using) dozens of patterns, you can make each song sound unique, as it should, and also tailor the patterns to the songs. A very sad lament, for example, shouldn't have a bouncy "oom pah pah" bass pattern.

Listen to all your patterns, and use them carefully, and your arrangements will shine.

SYLVIA'S FAVORITE PATTERN

I'd like to share one of my favorite patterns with you. It may look a bit complex at first, but once you get used to it, it is extremely versatile and can be used in all sorts of pieces. I start with this basic pattern of the root, the 5th, and the 3rd way up on top. Be sure your thumb is playing the 3rd of the chord, not an octave of the root.

The next step is to keep what you already had, and add the root note an octave higher like this:

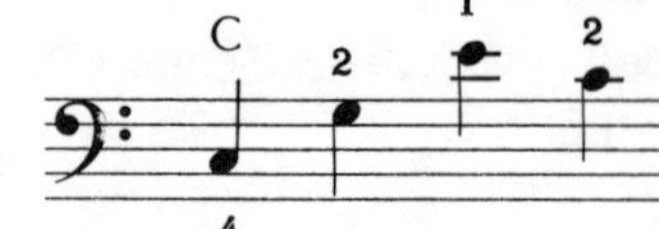

If we want to keep building on this pattern, we'd next add the 5th of the chord again on top:

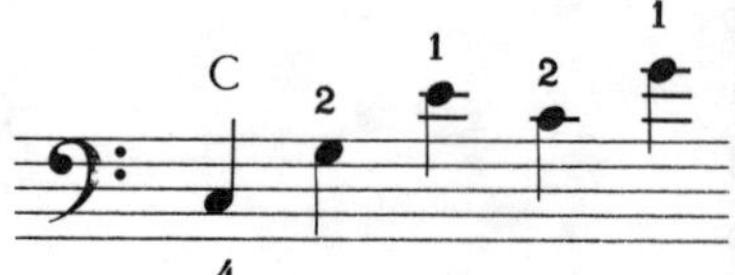

We can continue in this manner all the way up the harp. By the way, this complete pattern is a great way to end a piece.

This pattern comes in handy in lots of situations. Use as many of the notes as you want, in whatever rhythm you want. For example, go back to "Silent Night" and try some of these patterns. (You may want to move the melody up an octave, to give you room.) Notice that some of the patterns last for 2 measures.

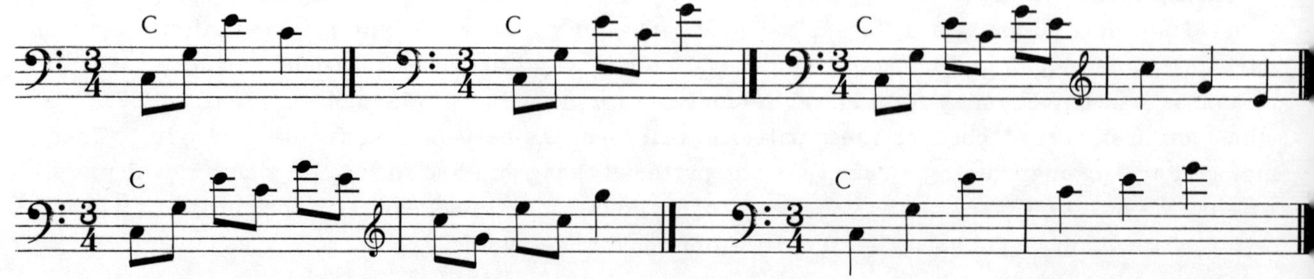

Chapter 14 - Right Hand Chords

Did you ever wonder why the sopranos always get to sing the melody in the choir? If you ever ıng alto, as I did, or tenor or bass, you hardly ever got to sing the "easy part", the melody; you ways had to learn the "harder parts". Why is this?

One reason is that we tend to hear the highest note as the melody. If you heard a choir sing a song ou had never heard before, and all four voices were of equal volume and relatively equal impor- ınce, you would probably assume that the highest note was the melody.

This concept of the highest note being the melody is extremely important in the next step in mak- ıg your arrangements sound full and interesting. This next step is to add chords to your right and along with the melody. Try playing this example as written, and see if you can figure out hat the tune is.

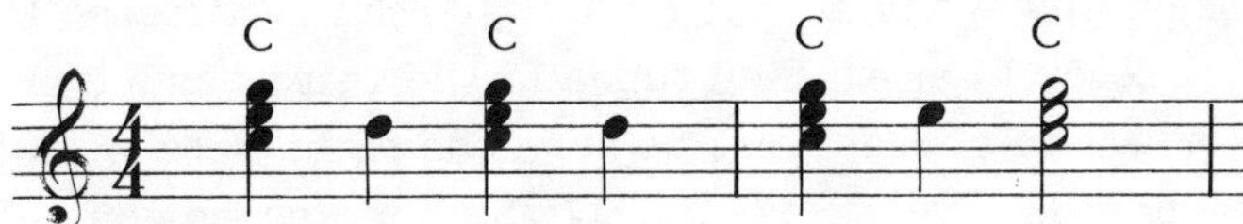

id that sound familiar? No? Well, you've been singing that song since you were 2 years old. That as "Mary Had a Little Lamb"! It didn't sound much like it, did it? That is because we didn't keep ıe melody on top when we added the chords. Now try it like this:

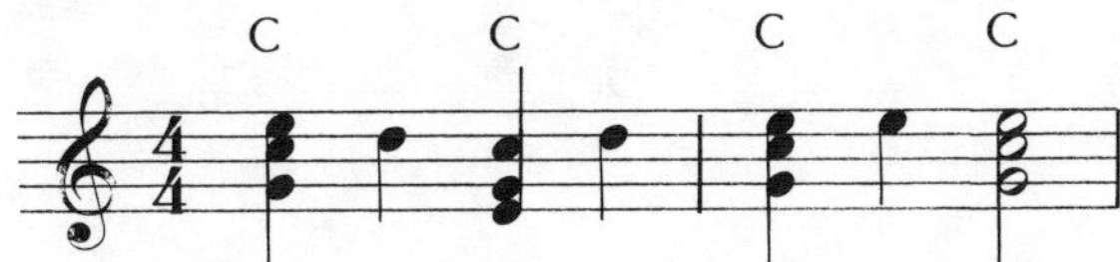

ow, that sounds better, doesn't it! So, you can see (and hear) that when you are adding chords to ıe melody in the right hand, you must be very careful to use the proper inversion of the chord that ill keep the melody on top. Another way of thinking of this is that whenever you play a chord in our right hand, the melody will be played with your THUMB.

Up until now, we have been talking about chord inversions by what note is on the bottom (the ass). Now, it is important to think about what note is on the TOP of the inversion.

Let's start with a song we did early in this book, "Down in the Valley." We're going to add a chord ı the right hand on the first beat of each measure.

OWN IN THE VALLEY

Look at the first three measures of "Down in the Valley". They all use a C chord. However, wh we add the chords to the right hand on the first beat of each measure, each of these C chords will in a different inversion, like this:

Looking at these inversions by what note is on TOP (which is dictated by the melody), the first chord has a G on top, the second has an E on top, and the third has a C on top. (It doesn't matter you use 3-note chords or 4-note chords; just be sure the right note is on top.)

Now let's look at the G chords. The first G chord (which is tied, so you only play it once), has a D top, then a G chord with a G on top, and then two G chords with Gs on top.

Sometimes the melody note is not actually a note that is in the chord. For example, notice th the last G chord in "Down in the Valley" has an F on top (measure #10), but there isn't an F in a chord! That's ok, just keep the F on top, and play a G chord underneath it, making a G7 chord:

Just remember to keep the melody on top, and then add the chords below.

DOWN IN THE VALLEY

This next song from Ireland has several names: "Coulin Dhas", "Mo Bouchaleen Bwee", or "M Yellow-haired Lad". I've written it out two ways. The first way is with just the melody and th chords. The second is an example of adding the chords in the right hand. Notice that I've put chord in the right hand on the first beat of every measure and also whenever a new chord comes i even if that is in the middle of a measure. Also I add extra chords in the right hand in the middle some measures just because I think they'll sound good there.

Play through this second version several times, being sure you understand how I came up with the notes in the right hand chords. Once you understand it, read the first version and add chords to the right on the downbeats, and when the chords change, and whenever you think they are appropriate.

Once you have the right hand and the chords figured out, make a nice arrangement for your left hand.

COULIN DHAS or MY YELLOW-HAIRED LAD

Let's try another song we learned earlier in this book, "Farewell to Tarwathie". I'll write it out again so it is here on this page for you. Once again, we'll add chords to the right hand on the first beat of each measure.

FAREWELL TO TARWATHIE

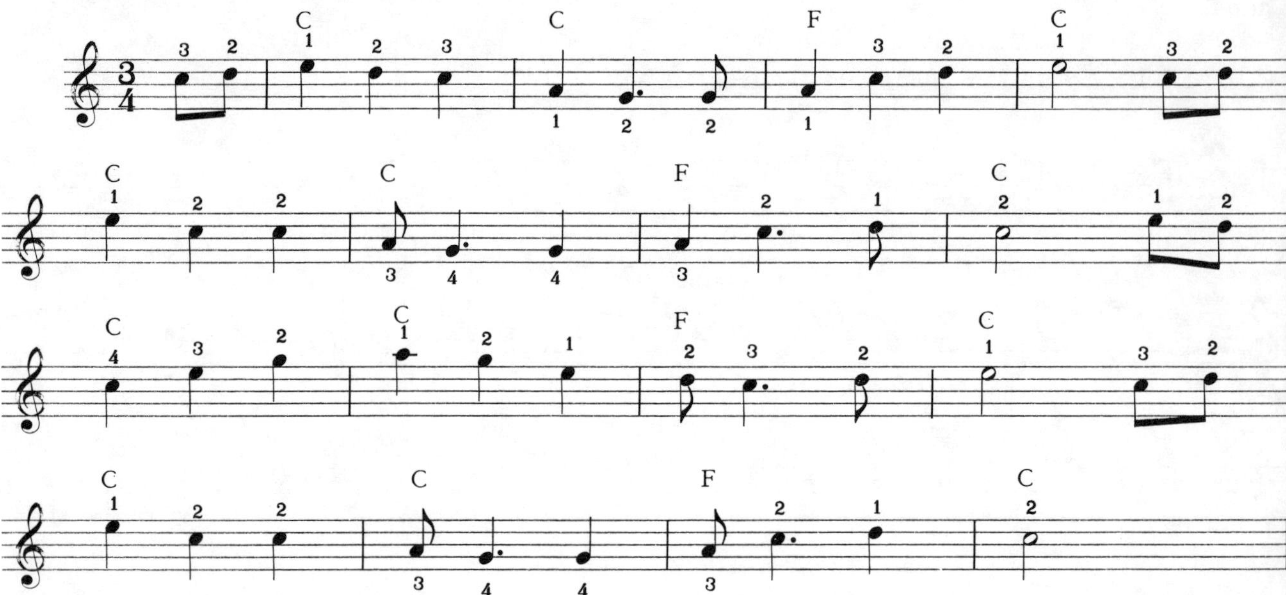

"Farewell to Tarwathie" has several examples of melody notes that are not in the chord. Look at the 2nd full measure, which should be a C chord. The melody starts the measure on an A (which is not in a C chord), but then drops down one note to a G (which is in a C chord). There are two ways you could play this chord when you add the chord to the right hand:

In this example, the first chord has become a C6 and may sound a little dissonant because of the G and A strings right together, but it still works fine. However, I think the best choice in this instance is the second one, since the A of the melody will move down to the G in the next beat, anyway. So, you could play that measure like this:

That same pattern of a C chord with an A note in the melody happens three more times in the piece, including once (in measure #10) an octave higher.

There's another place in "Farewell to Tarwathie" that has a similar problem. Look at the 11th measure that has an F chord, with a D note (which is not in an F chord) in the melody. Once again, the second note goes down one string to a note that is in the F chord, so we can treat it the same way we treated the earlier measures, like this:

F

Now try playing "Farewell to Tarwathie" adding chords to the right hand on the first beat of each measure. You can still keep any left hand patterns that you used before, and add them to this newly expanded right hand. Notice that the melody fingerings will all be different than they were before because of your chords.

"Silent Night" sounds very good with chords in the right hand. Notice that I have moved the melody up an octave to keep it out of the way of the left hand. I have written in the chords for the first line to get you started. Add chords in the right hand to the rest of the melody. You should be able to keep your same left hand inversions and arrangements that you have used before.

SILENT NIGHT

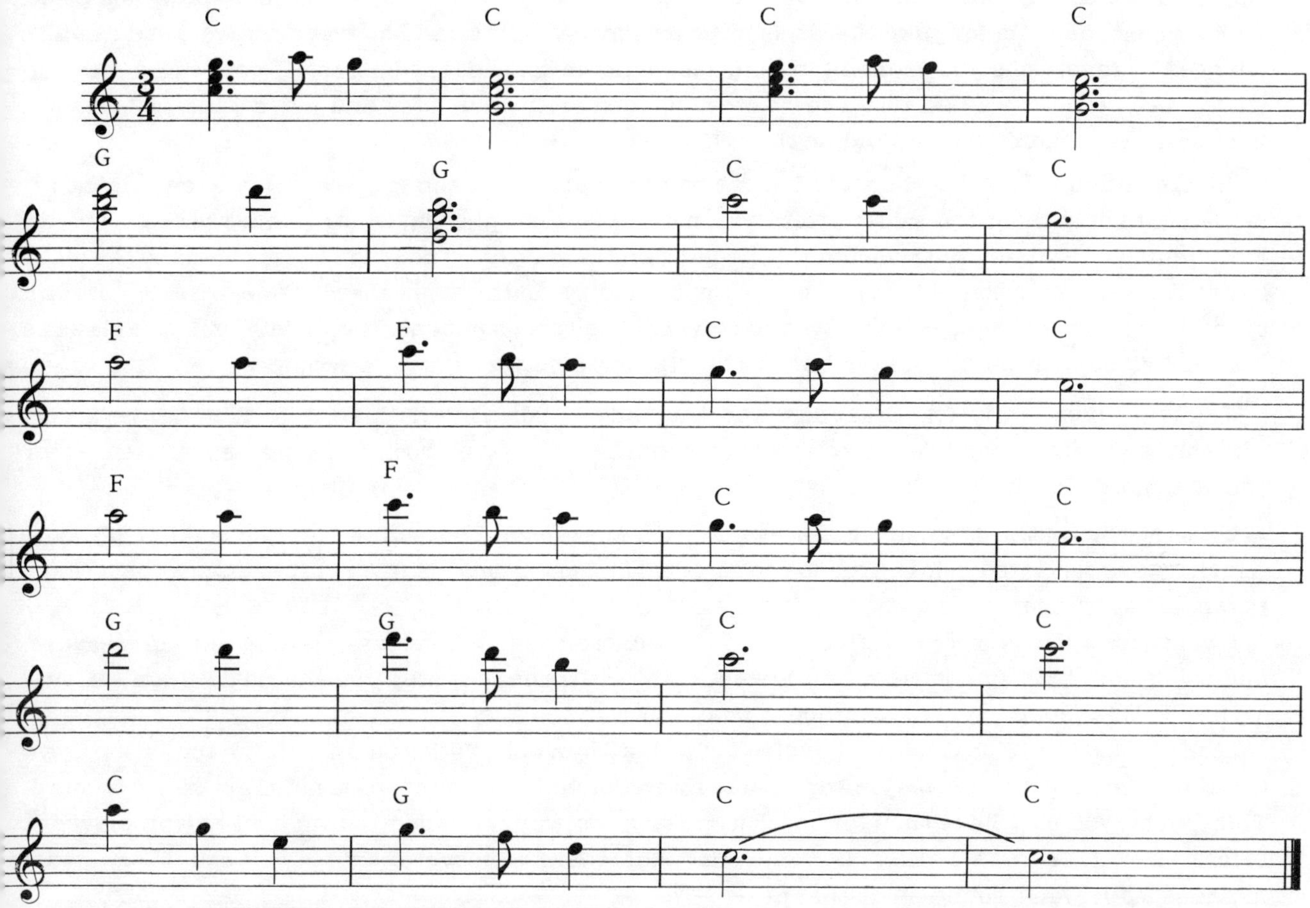

Let's try adding right hand chords to this "Welsh Carol". Notice that sometimes the chord changes in the middle of the measure. Whenever you have a chord indicated, play that chord with your right hand, BEING SURE YOU KEEP THE MELODY ON THE TOP OF THE CHORD. A few of the F chords have non-chord melody notes. Treat them the same way you did in "Farewell to Tarwathie".

Once you've practiced adding the chords in the right hand, finish your arrangement by adding an accompaniment with your left hand.

A WELSH CAROL

Try playing some of the other songs you have been working on in this book, and add chords to the right hand. You can do this on the first beat of each measure, or when the chords change, or whenever you think it would sound good.

In general, when adding the chords to the right, you can keep the left hand accompaniment just the way you had it. Sometimes, however, your two hands will "run into each other" if you do it this way. When this happens, you can move your right hand up an octave throughout the whole piece, which gives you room for your chords, or perhaps move the left hand down an octave. You can also change the inversions you're using in your left hand on some of the chords. If your hands are getting in each other's way on just a few notes, you can alter your left hand notes a bit, or leave out part or all of a chord in one hand or the other.

This technique of adding chords to the melody in your right hand is a great way to enrich the arrangements of some of the easier pieces you may have been playing in other harp books, as well. First, you need to figure out what chord the left hand is playing. Then, add these chords to the right hand. (It really does sound better if both hands are playing the same chord! Otherwise, it sounds a bit bizarre!) You will now have a new and more exciting arrangement. For variety, you can play the "easier" version through once, and then the "fuller" arrangement as a second verse.

My arrangements of "The Grenadier and the Lady", "My Love is Like A Red, Red Rose", and "Greensleeves" from the "Teach Yourself To Play the Folk Harp" book work well as written when you add chords to the right hand.

Let's try this on the Scottish air "Farewell" from my "Teach Yourself to Play the Folk Harp" book, which I have reprinted below. This is the same arrangement that is in the book, except that I have taken out the fingering and the brackets.

I went through the piece and figured out what chord the left hand was playing in each measure, and wrote the chord symbol above each measure. This is the first step you should do when starting a piece with a left hand accompaniment that you want to keep.

Look at measure 15 that has an * instead of a chord symbol. Notice that the left hand is playing a G chord. The right hand is playing an A note and a C note. Neither of these notes are in the G chord. This is why you may have thought that this measure always sounded "funny" when you played it before. Now that we're adding chords to the right, there are several things you can do with this measure, so it won't sound so dissonant.

#1. Play the measure exactly as written, and DON'T add a chord to the right. That way it will just sound as "funny" as it always did.
#2. Change the chord in the left to an F chord, instead of a G chord, by moving each note in the left down one note. Then add an F chord to the right hand as well.

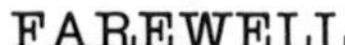

G
Am
F
C
Am
F
*
C
C
Am
F
C
C
Am
C/E
F
F
C
Am
Em
F
C
G
C
C

Chapter 15 - Counter-Melodies

An accompaniment does not always have to be chordal. Sometimes you can use a melodic accompaniment, instead. A countermelody, or descant, is a melodic line that sounds good when played against the main melody. One example would be in a duet or a choir. If the sopranos are singing the main melody, the altos are probably singing a countermelody.

The easiest countermelodies are formed by following the melody an interval of either a 3rd lower than the melody, or a 6th lower. This type of countermelody is called parallel motion.

For example, let's try it on a lullaby from France, "Fais Do-Do" (which means "Go To Sleep"). But first, you should play the melody through a few times with the chords in your left, so you become familiar with the melody. (Don't forget to sharp all your F's, since this piece is in the key of G!)

FAIS DO-DO - VERSION #1

G G D G

G Em C D 1 G

2 G * G D G D

G D G D

G G D G

G Em C D G

Now, we'll try some countermelodies in parallel motion. This time, ignore the chord indications. Just as an example, we're going to start with the middle section of the piece (marked with an * on the music). Play the melody with your right hand, and with your left hand, play notes a 3rd lower, like this: (The notes with the stems up are for your right hand, with the stems down for your left.)

example "A"

It is a little easier if we lower the left hand an octave from where it was, making it an "octave plus a 3rd" lower, like this:

example "B"

Doesn't that sound nice? Now, try it on the beginning of the piece, like this.

example "C"

That didn't sound quite as good as the other section did. Somehow the harmony wasn't quite right. Let's try that first line again, and this time, we'll make the countermelody an interval of a 6th lower than the melody.

example "D"

In that line, a 6th lower sounded much better than a 3rd lower did. Let's now go back and try the middle section (*) that we liked with a 3rd lower (examples A and B), and see what they sound like a 6th lower.

example "E"

Oh dear! That sounded pretty strange. In that passage, the 3rd lower we did before sounded much better.

Now go back to Version #1 of "Fais Do-Do" and try the whole piece. Play the beginning with the left a 6th lower (example D), the middle section (*) an "octave plus a 3rd" lower (example B), and the last part like the beginning (a 6th lower). Try to just do it out of your head, looking at the music in Version #1, instead of looking at the examples I wrote out.

If you played it correctly, that should have sounded very nice. But why does the countermelody sometimes sound good a 3rd lower, and sometimes it sounds better a 6th lower. And why did we pick those intervals, instead of a 2nd lower or a 4th lower or something like that?

The answer to these questions has to do with chords. When you're playing these countermelodies, you're forming small two-note chords; and since chords are made up of intervals of 3rds, these sound the best. If you invert an interval of a 3rd, you come up with an interval of a 6th; for example, this is a 3rd:

and this is a 6th:

They are the same notes, just in a different order. That's why 6ths often work as well as 3rds.

And now for the reason why sometimes a 3rd lower sounds better, and sometimes a 6th lower sounds better. A lot of it depends on where the melody note falls in the chord. For example, if the melody note is the root of the chord (i.e. the melody is a C, and the chord is a C chord), if you played a 3rd lower it would be an A note, which is not in a C chord, so it may not sound as good.

However, if you played a 6th lower, an E note, that IS in the C chord, so it should sound better.

Instead of getting too technical and "thinking" too much, though, the best way is just to try it either way, and see which one you like better.

And now for a small hint. Another way to think about which note is a 6th lower, is to actually think a 3rd higher and then go down an octave. For example, if the melody note is C, a 6th lower would be E. Or, another way to look at it is a 3rd higher than C is also E, and you just play it an octave lower so that the melody stays the highest note. Whichever way you think about it, you should come up with the same answer. This is because, as we learned a minute ago, if you invert an interval of a 3rd, you'll get a 6th (and vice versa).

CONTRARY MOTION

So far, when we have added a countermelody, we have been playing in parallel motion with our two hands, both of them going the same direction at the same time. But sometimes it sounds really nice to go OPPOSITE DIRECTIONS with your two hands, which is called CONTRARY MOTION. Any of you who have played in my "Teach Yourself to Play the Folk Harp" book will remember Beethoven's "Ode to Joy" from Lesson 4 which I am reprinting here. Notice how sometimes the two hands go the same direction an "octave and a 3rd" apart (measures 1, 5, and 13), and sometimes they go in opposite directions (measures 3, 7, and 15). This gives the piece some variety. Also, the countermelodies do not continue straight through the entire piece: they last one measure, and then there is a measure of another type of accompaniment. These "breaks" help give the ear a rest from the same harmonies.

ODE TO JOY

When experimenting with contrary motion, start your countermelody on one of the notes of the chord, and go in the opposite direction from the melody. If that doesn't work well, try starting on a different note of the chord. You may need to skip a note here and there in your countermelody to make it sound good.

With this new knowledge, let's see what else we can do with "Fais Do-Do" to give it more variety. Here's an arrangement that I made using parallel motion, contrary motion, and some miscellaneous chord notes. Analyze the left hand and try to figure out what I did in each measure, and why I did it. Which notes are a 3rd lower than the melody? Which ones are a 6th lower? Where did I use parallel motion? Where did I use contrary motion? Where did I add "extra" notes? How did I change it when the same melody came in more than once? Really examine this piece and use it to get new ideas for your arrangements.

FAIS DO-DO #2

Now you're ready to try your own arrangements using countermelodies in these next pieces. Don't use parallel motion and contrary motion throughout the entire piece, just in the places where it sounds really good. The rest of the time, use any of the chordal patterns you've already learned in this book.

Good places to try parallel and contrary motion are in scale type passages of several notes that move from one string to the next adjacent string.

Parallel motion or contrary motion do not have to be strictly adhered to. For example, if you find a passage that sounds really good in parallel motion except for one note, just change that one note in your left to something that sounds better.

"The Smiling Spring" is Scottish, "The Little Sandman" is Dutch, and "Shepherds, Leave Your Crooks" is a Christmas carol from France.

Good luck! Here we go!

THE SMILING SPRING

THE LITTLE SANDMAN
SHEPHERDS, LEAVE YOUR CROOKS

Chapter 16 - Modes

With our harps tuned with no sharps or flats, we can easily play in the keys of C or A minor. Even though these two keys use the exact same notes, the pieces that are in the key of C (based on the C major scale and with an emphasis on the C major chord), sound very different from the pieces in the key of A minor (based on the A minor scale with an emphasis on the A minor chord). If we build scales on notes other than C or A, and don't add any sharps or flats, we come up with scales that are called "modes". Modes were very popular in medieval times, and have survived to the present day. In fact, our major and minor scales are types of modes, themselves. Our major scale can be called the Ionian Mode, and the natural minor scale can be called the Aeolian Mode.

This chart shows the seven most common modes, and we will be dealing with two of them in this book. (The "‿"s indicate the half-steps.)

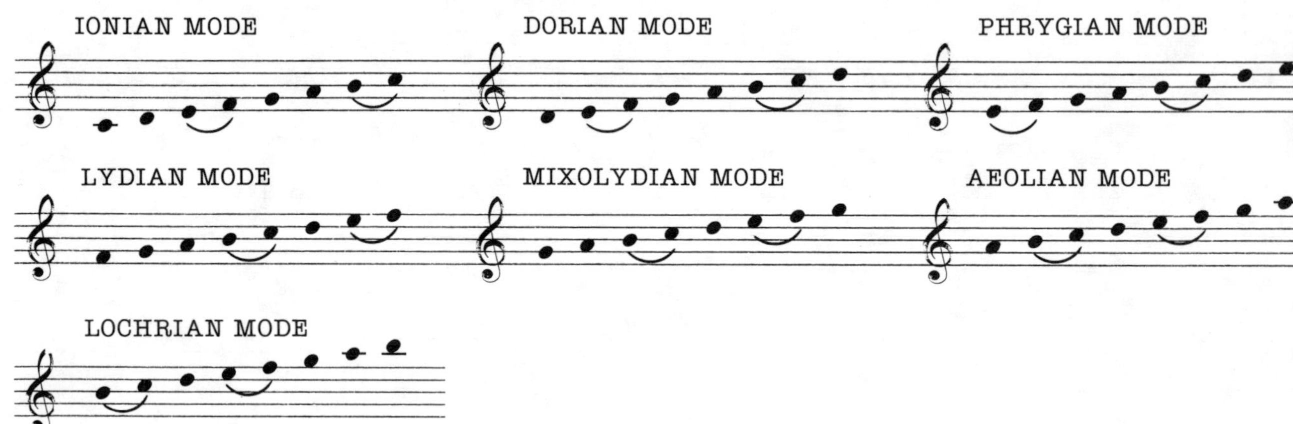

(If you ever have to memorize the names of these modes for a music theory class, a good mnemonic device for their order is: "I Don't Particularly Like Many Arctic Lands.")

Two modes that are still common in folk music are the Dorian mode, and the Mixolydian mode. We'll begin with the Dorian mode.

The Dorian mode is based on a D note, and has a minor flavor since its main chord is a Dm. It differs from the KEY of Dm, however, since in the key of Dm the B note is a B flat, whereas in the Dorian mode the B note is a B natural. It is this B natural that gives the Dorian mode its characteristic sound.

These next three pieces from England and Ireland are all in the Dorian mode. Play through them and make your own arrangements. Get used to the distinctive sound of the Dorian mode.

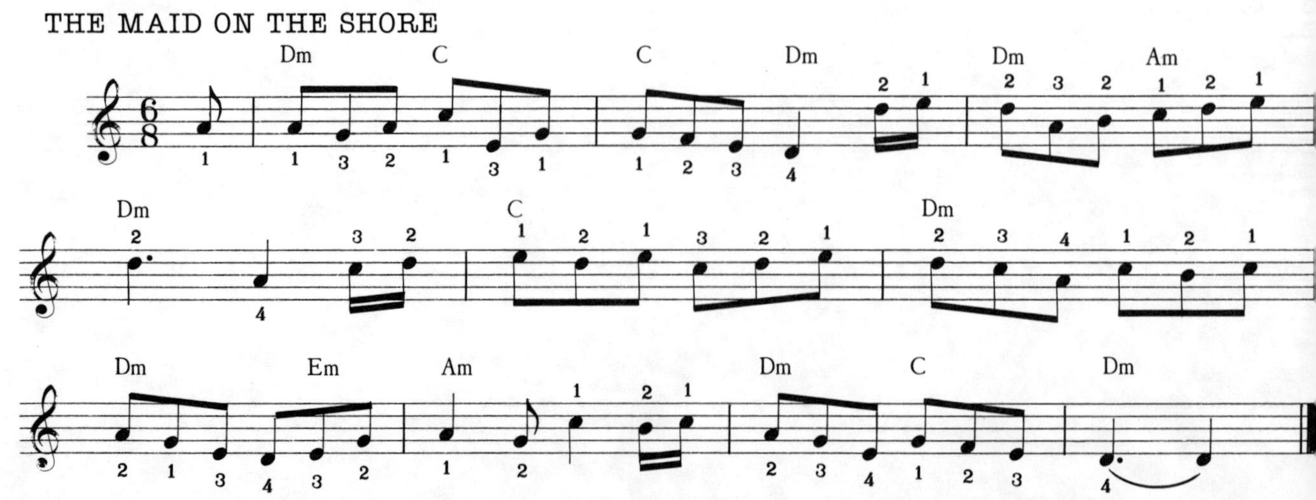

ARBOROUGH FAIR

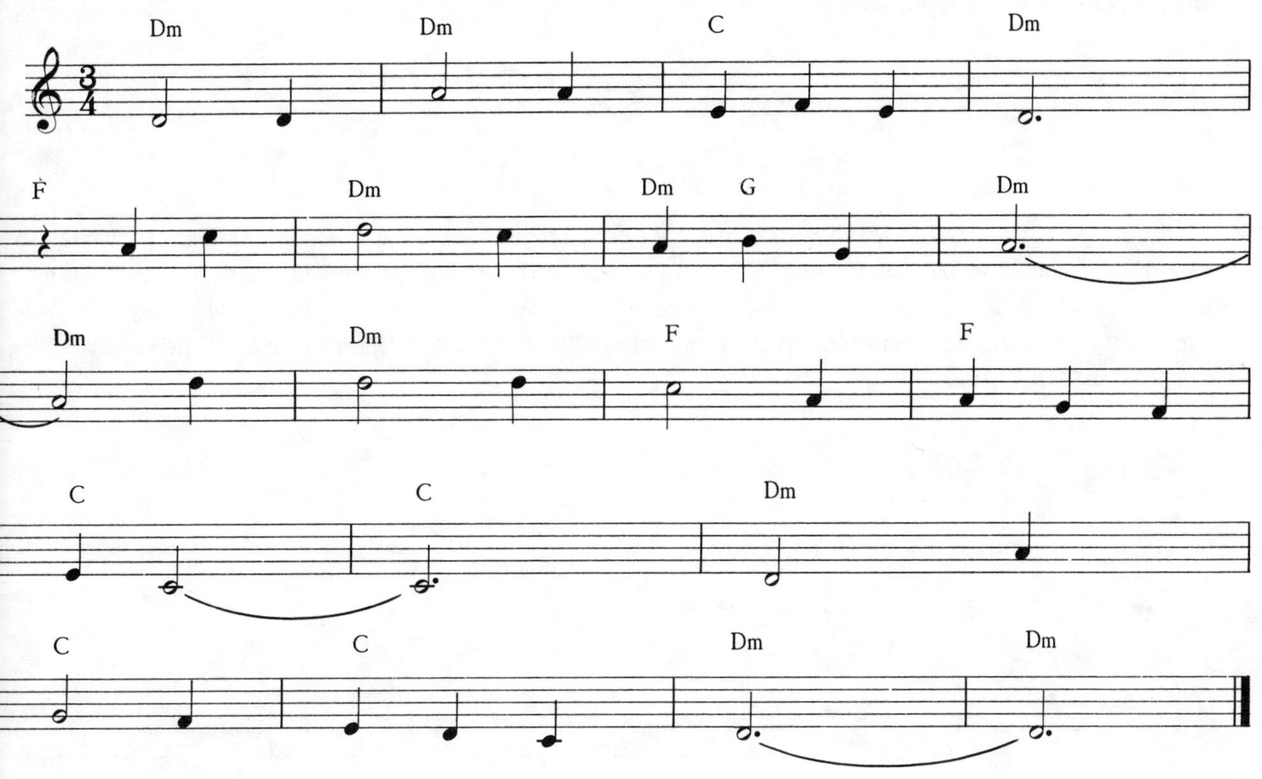

HE NEXT MARKET DAY

Another popular mode in folk music is the Mixolydian mode. When we're tuned with no sharps flats, the Mixolydian mode is based on G.

MIXOLYDIAN MODE

The note that gives the Mixolydian mode its characteristic sound is the F natural. (If it was in t key of G major, it would be an F#.) Notice in these next two pieces that the predominant chords a G major (which is the note the mode is based on), and F major (the chord that emphasizes t "modality" the most). "She Moved Thro' The Fair" is an ancient Irish air, and "The Great Silkie" an old English ballad.

SHE MOVED THROUGH THE FAIR

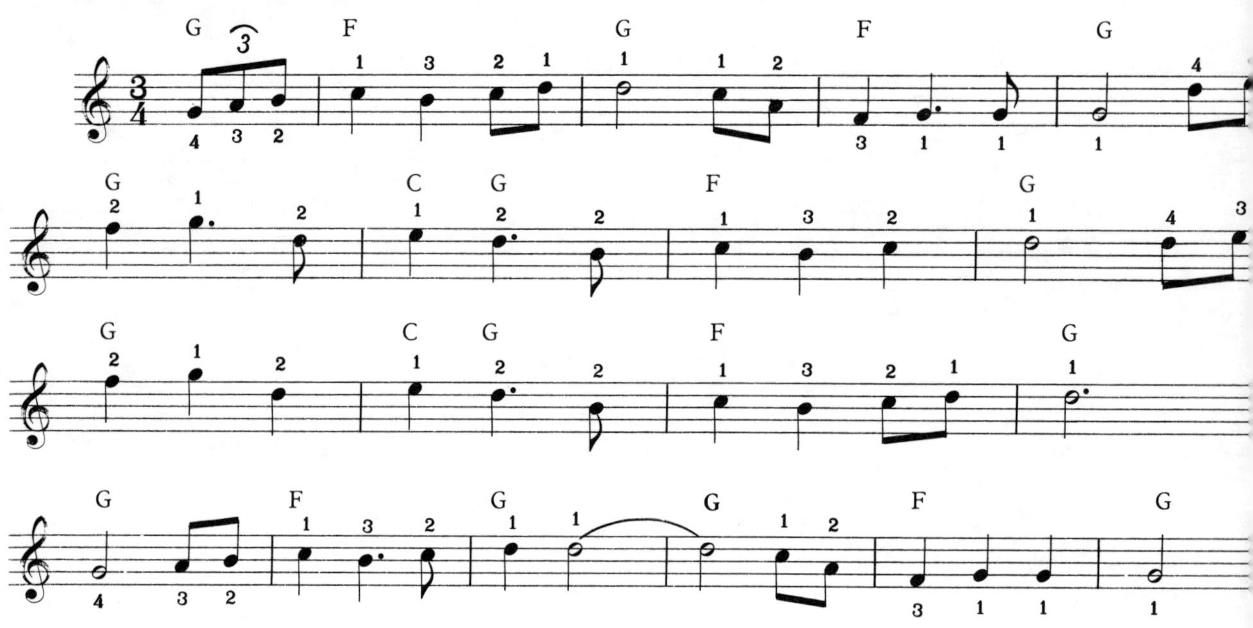

THE GREAT SILKIE

So far, we have played the modes with our harps tuned with no sharps or flats. However, modes can be played in other tunings as well. If we consider that we've been tuned to a C major scale, the Dorian mode started on the second note of the scale (the D note), and the Mixolydian mode started on the 5th note of the C major scale (the G).

It therefore seems logical that if we tune our harps to the key of G major (by sharping our F's) the modes will keep the same relationship. The Dorian mode will start on the 2nd note of the G major scale (which is an A note), and the Mixolydian note will start on the 5th note of the G major scale (which is a D).

Sharp all your F's and play these modal tunes. "The Hills of Glenshee" (Dorian) is from Scotland, and "On Board the Kangaroo" (Mixolydian) is an Irish sea shanty.

THE HILLS OF GLENSHEE

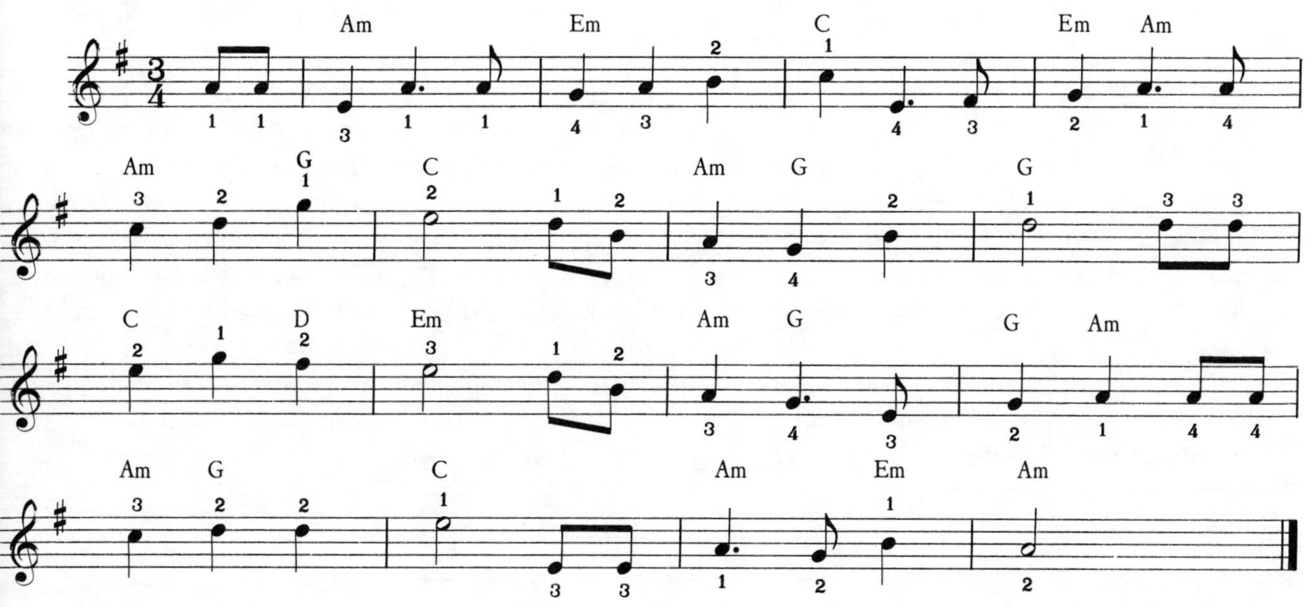

ON BOARD THE KANGAROO

Chapter 17 - "Neutral Chords"

Earlier in this book, at the end of Chapter 6, we started a discussion about "neutral chords". I said that if the music calls for a major chord, and your harp is tuned to a key where the chord is minor (or vice versa), that you could play a "neutral chord". I defined a "neutral chord" as a chord where you leave out the 3rd (the middle note), so the ear can't tell whether it is major or minor. (By the way, the name "neutral chord" is not an official musical term, it is one I made up to describe this type of chord. Another name for it is a "modal chord".)

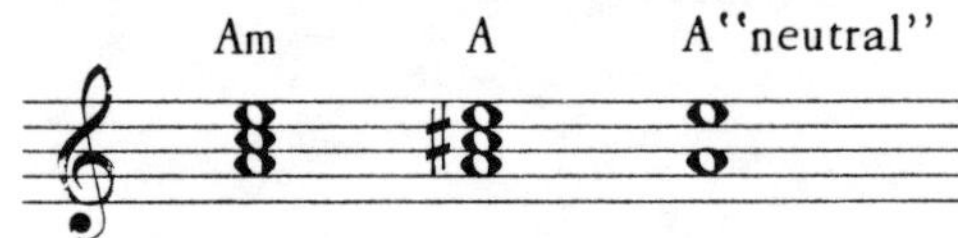

Look at the music for the Slovakian song "Goodnight" below. It is in the key of A minor. Normally in this tuning our E chord would be E minor. However, if you look at the E chords in this piece, you'll notice that they are all E major. OK, we could sharp our G's, which would give us E major chords. However, we'd then be in trouble in the melody of the 3rd line, where there is a G natural in the melody. Also, it would ruin the G major and C major chords. So, in this instance, it might be a good idea to try "E neutral" chords. Whenever you come to an E chord, leave out the G note; just play E notes and B notes. (That is, you leave out the 3rd of the chord, and just play the root and the 5th.)

I have come up with a shorthand way of indicating places in the music where I want to play a "neutral chord". I just circle the name of the chord, and that tells me that I need to leave out the 3rd of the chord. Notice that I circled all the E chords in this piece.

GOODNIGHT

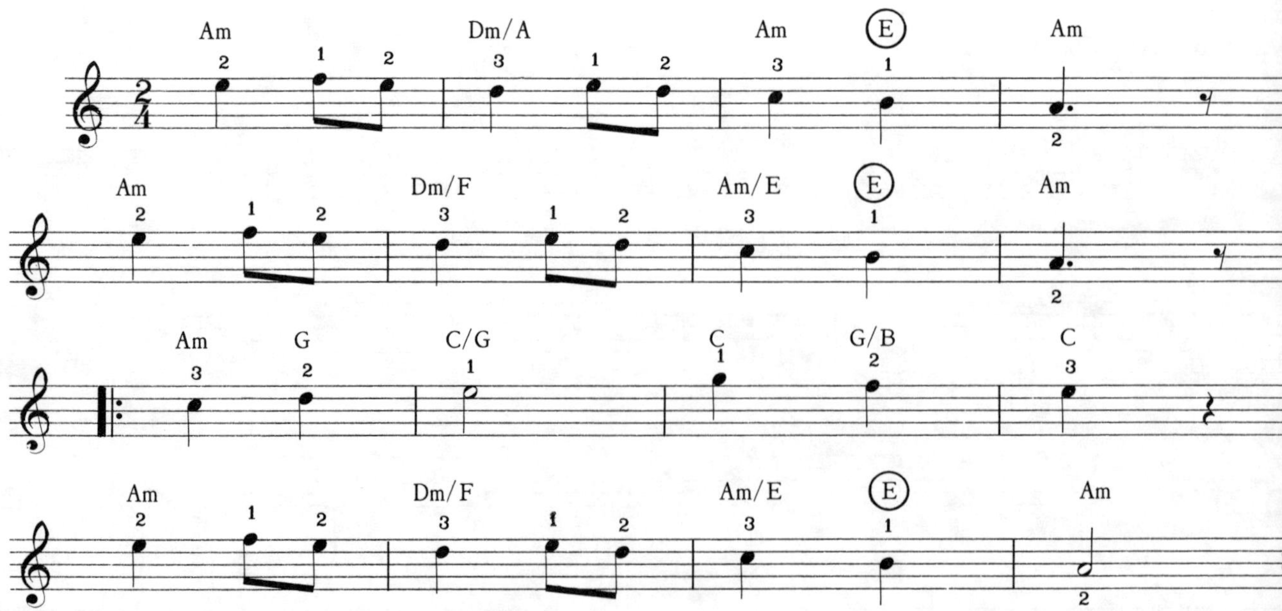

"Take Me, Earth" (a song from Russia) has several chords which we need to discuss. Like the previous piece, it is in the key of A minor, but it has E major chords instead of E minor chords. However, in this instance, they are E7 chords. We can still make them "neutral" by leaving out the G notes, but since they are 7th chords, we can add D notes. So, for these E7 chords you will play E, B, and D notes.

This piece also has both A minor chords (which are ok), and A major chords (which we need to make "neutral"). Once again, these A major chords actually are A7. So, for these A7 chords you can play A, E, and G notes (just leave out the C). The A minor chords can be played in the normal way.

There is one more strange chord in this piece: Dm6/F. The Dm6 chord contains the notes D, F, A, and B (the D minor chord plus the 6th which is B). Play it in the inversion with the F note on the bottom (F, A, B, D).

TAKE ME, EARTH

Chapter 18 - Tuning Your Harp To Two Keys At Once

There are several kinds of minor scales. If your harp is tuned with no sharps or flats (the key of C major or A minor) the scale from A to A is called the "natural minor scale". It has half-steps between the 2nd and 3rd notes, and between the 5th and 6th notes; like this.

A NATURAL MINOR SCALE

Another example is in the key of E minor, the E natural minor scale is:

E NATURAL MINOR SCALE

There is another kind of minor scale, and it uses notes that are not in the key signature. The "harmonic minor scale" raises the 7th note of the natural minor scale by one half-step. This gives us a skip of 1½ steps between the 6th and 7th notes, with half-steps between the 2nd and 3rd notes, the 5th and 6th notes, and also the 7th and 8th notes.

A HARMONIC MINOR SCALE

E HARMONIC MINOR SCALE

It is not uncommon to find pieces written in the key of A minor with lots of G#s thrown in. This is because these pieces are based on a "harmonic minor scale" instead of a "natural minor scale." The problem with playing these pieces on the folk harp is that you need to have some "G sharps", but you also need some "G naturals" if you want to also play C major chords, G major chords, or E minor chords.

Sometimes these G#s only show up in the chords, as they did in the two pieces in Chapter 17, but sometimes they are in the melody, as well. If the sharps are in the melody, just using "neutral chords" cannot fix everything.

The way to solve this problem on the folk harp is to tune some of the G's on your harp natural, and tune some of them sharp (with your sharping lever, or your tuning key). We'll try this on the French recipe song, "Fish Godiveau". (I call it a "recipe song" since the words explain how to prepare Godiveau, a dish of dough with creamed fish.)

First of all, notice that the G above middle C is sharped throughout the melody. So, you'll need to sharp that G on your harp. However, if we look at the chords, we'll see that we need a C chord, and a G chord; both of which need G naturals. Therefore, we'll leave the G BELOW middle C as a G natural.

Look at the E major chords where I have circled the name of the chord. E major chords, of course, need a G#. I have circled these chords to remind me that I can't play a G note in my left hand in these chords, because my G below middle C is tuned as a NATURAL. Therefore, as we learned in the last chapter, I need to make these chords "neutral" in my left hand, by leaving out the G. However, if you look at the melody in each of those measures, you'll notice that the melody will play the G# on the next note, anyway, so the chord will sound major, as it should.

I have written out a sample accompaniment for this piece so you can see how this works. I added a countermelody in the second line for some variety. Notice that the only G's I used in the left hand were G naturals; I left out the G#'s in the E major chords in the left hand.

Experiment with other accompaniments to this piece, so you get used to which notes to leave out. Try adding chords to the right hand, but be careful about your G's and G#'s!

FISH GODIVEAU

Here's another French piece, "The Watermen", with a similar problem. Once again, you'll tune the G ABOVE middle C to a G# and leave the G BELOW middle C a G natural.

Look at the E major chords at the end of the first two lines. In my arrangement I added the G# in the RIGHT HAND to fill out the chord, since I couldn't add it in the left hand.

Play through my arrangement, paying close attention to what I did with all the G's. Then try your own arrangement. Just remember to leave the G note out of the E major chords in your left hand, otherwise you'll accidentally make them E minor chords, which will sound awful with the G# in the melody!

THE WATERMEN

Now you're ready to do one all on your own. For "The Jolly Miller", a song from New England, you can keep your harp tuned exactly the same way as you did on the last two pieces, with one G# and one G natural. I have circled the E major chords where you'll have to be sure the *left hand* chords are neutral.

THE JOLLY MILLER

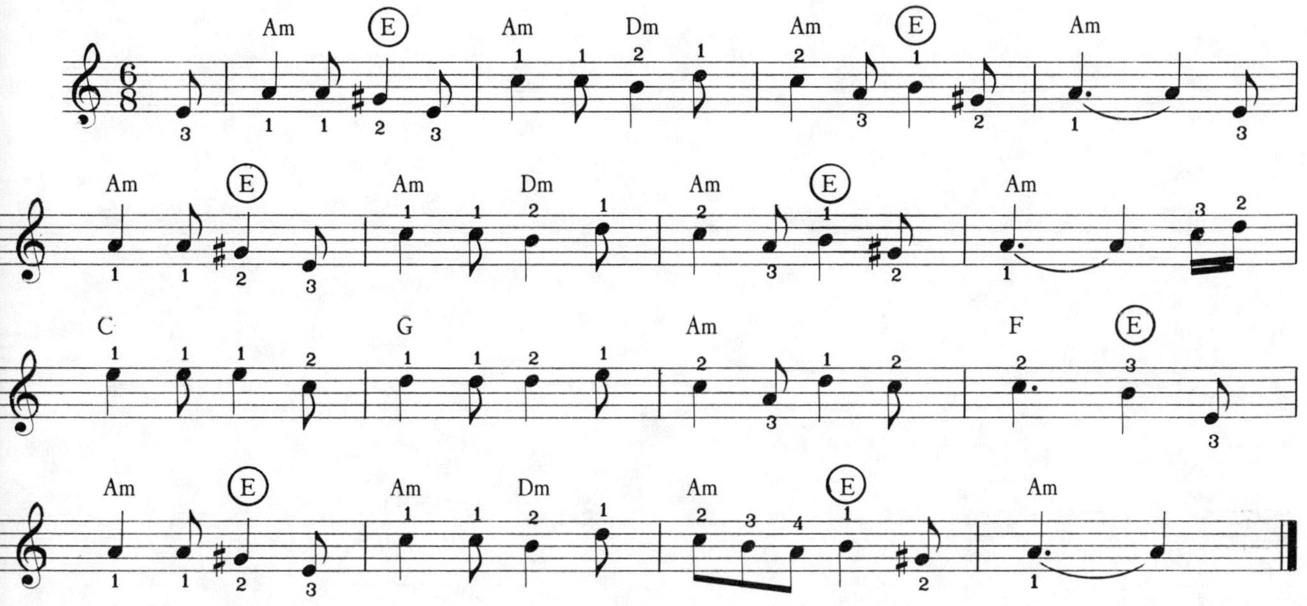

To play "The Three Ravens" (an old English ballad) and "The Marsh of Rhuddlan" (from Wales), you can leave your harp tuned the same way as the last three songs, but you must be sure that the G "an-octave-and-a-half above middle C" is a G natural. In the previous pieces we never used this G, so it didn't matter how it was tuned. But in these next two pieces, we will need it, and it has to be a G natural.

If you add chords to the right hand of these pieces, be careful in the measures that have a C chord or a G chord. Be sure you don't put in the G# by mistake! Have fun!

THE THREE RAVENS

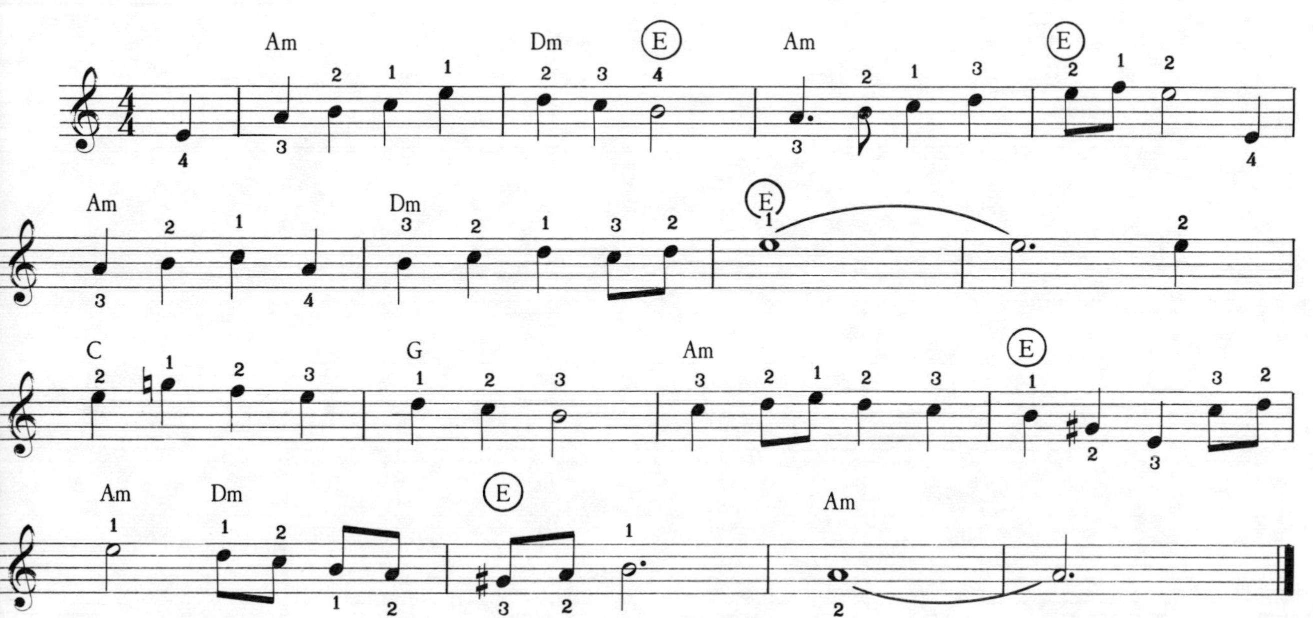

THE MARSH OF RHUDDLAN

Chapter 19 - Accidentals In The Melody

An accidental is a sharp, natural, or flat that departs from the key signature. That is, if you're playing along in the key of C and you suddenly get a G#, that is an accidental. Or, if you are in the key of G (which has F#s), and you suddenly see an F natural, that is an accidental.

When accidentals occur in the melody of a piece, they create problems for folk harpers. When this happens, you first need to decide whether the note is important to the melody. Sometimes the note with the accidental is not essential, and you can leave it out or change it to a different note and it won't drastically change the piece. Let's look at the following two-measure example. We're in the key of C, and we suddenly need an F#.

We have several options:

(a) Leave out the F# all together. This is usually the first thing to try, since it is the easiest.

(b) Change the F# to another note that is in the chord that you're using for that measure. For example, the chord for this first measure would probably be a C, so you could change the F# note to a C (as shown here), or an E.

(c) Notes that are on adjacent strings on the harp are sometimes called "neighbor tones". For example, an A is a "neighbor tone" to either G or B; a D is a "neighbor tone" to C or E; an F is a "neighbor tone" to either E or G, etc. Look at the note that is *immediately before* the F# that we need to change: it is a G. Our third choice is to try a "neighbor tone" to this G: either F natural or A. In this example I chose the A note, but the F natural might work just as well.

But sometimes the accidental is essential to the sound of the piece. The character of the piece would be altered if you left it out or changed it. In this instance, you must figure out a way to keep the note in your arrangement. Therefore, you'll need to use your sharping lever on that particular note, and then return it to a natural later in the piece. In our original example above, you'd have to be really speedy, since there is an F natural 2 notes before the F# and 3 notes after the F#. You'd have to make your arrangement so that you didn't need to play any notes in your left hand through that measure, so you could sharp and natural the F with your lever.

Look at the "Gartan Mother's Lullaby", a beautifully haunting song from Ireland. Notice that there is an F natural in the fourth-from-the-last measure. I would definitely consider this to be an important note in this song, and I wouldn't want to leave it out.

First, we need to figure out how much time we'll have to make the natural. Starting from the F natural, go BACKWARDS in the music until you get to an F in that same octave (which would be an F#). I found an F# two measures before the F natural. Therefore, sometime AFTER you play that F#, and BEFORE you get to the F natural, you'll have to disengage your sharping lever to make the string an F natural. That means that sometime in those two measures you have to have enough free time in your left hand to move up and change the lever. One suggestion would be to play the first C chord with all the notes of the chord at once instead of spreading them out in a kind of a pattern, which will give you time to get to your lever.

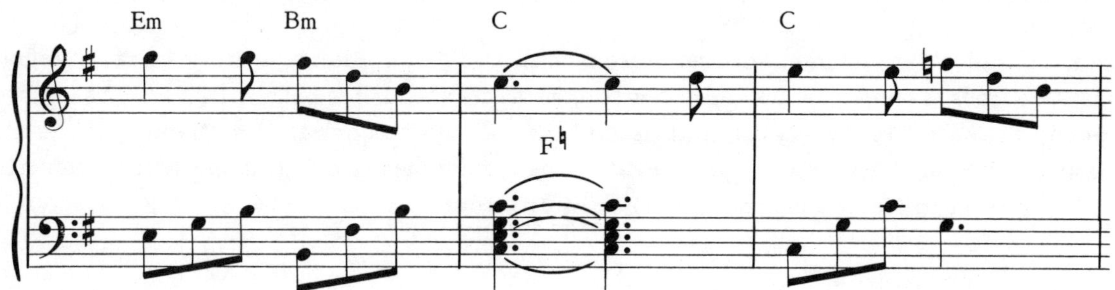

Or you could play part of the accompaniment with your right hand to keep the flow going. This still gives your left hand time to change the lever. And so, in the 2nd measure below you'd just play the low C note with your left hand, then the next three notes with your right hand.

Our next step is to figure out when we have to move the sharping lever back to an F#. Start at the F natural note, and continue reading through the piece until you get to the next F# in that same octave. Well, in this piece, we get lucky. There are no F#s in the melody in the rest of the piece. Therefore, it doesn't matter whether or not we sharp the F again. However, if you're going to repeat the piece, you'll have to be sure to sharp the F before you get to the 5th measure. Sometimes the best time to do this is right at the end of the piece, before you start over.

Now make an arrangement of "Gartan Mother's Lullaby" being sure to take care of the accidentals.

GARTAN MOTHER'S LULLABY

Chapter 20 - Substitute Chords

I'm sure you've noticed in music that it is common for the same melodic line to repeat more than once in a piece. Often when this happens it is nice to use different chords the second time the line is played.

For example, look at the popular French song "Auprès de ma Blonde". Notice that the melody of the first two lines is the same, but I did not use the same chords for both lines. Play the chords and the melody of these first two lines, and listen how the chords change the "flavor" of the melody.

Now play the last two lines. Once again, their melodies are the same (except for the last measures), but the different chords give them a different "flavor".

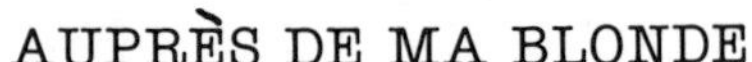

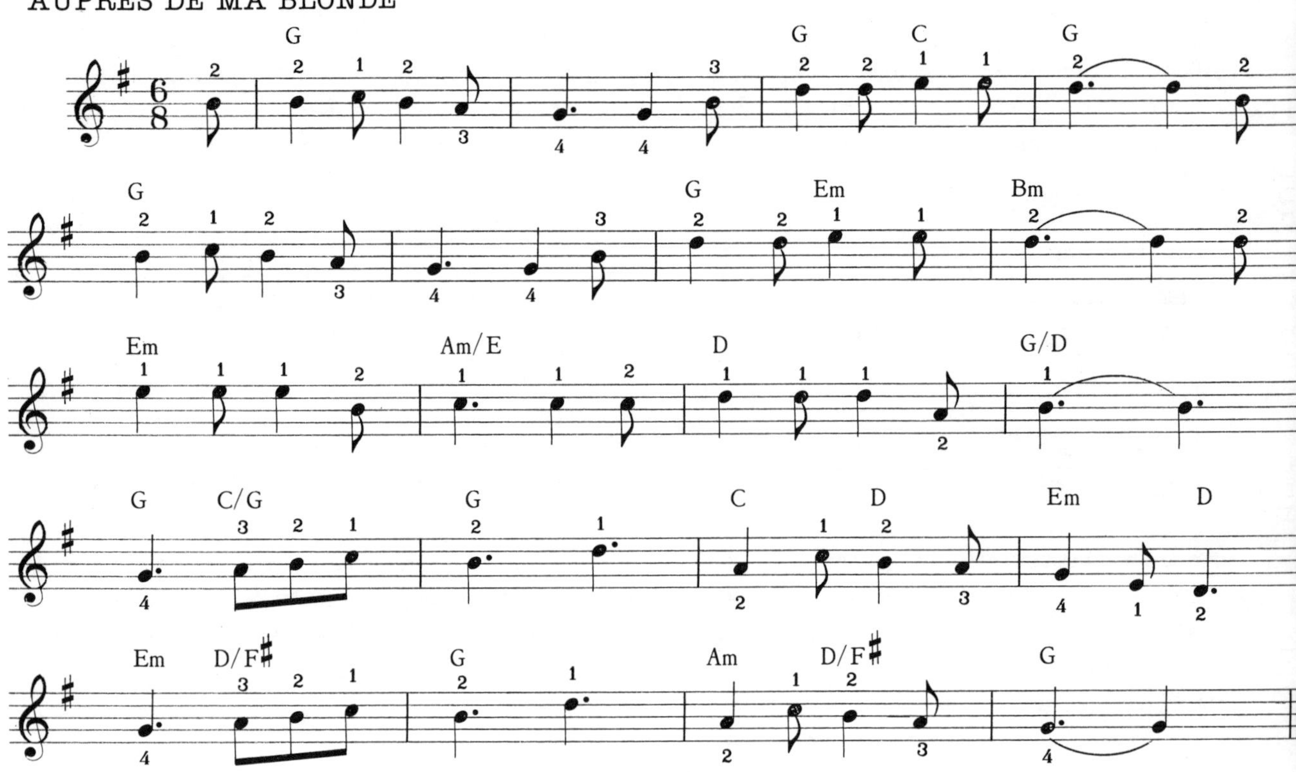

These are examples of using "substitute chords". That means that instead of using one chord, you can sometimes "substitute" a different chord.

Let's look at it from a different perspective. If you pick any chord, there are two other chords that share 2 of the same notes. For example, a C chord and an Am chord both contain C and E notes. And a C chord and an Em chord both share E and G notes.

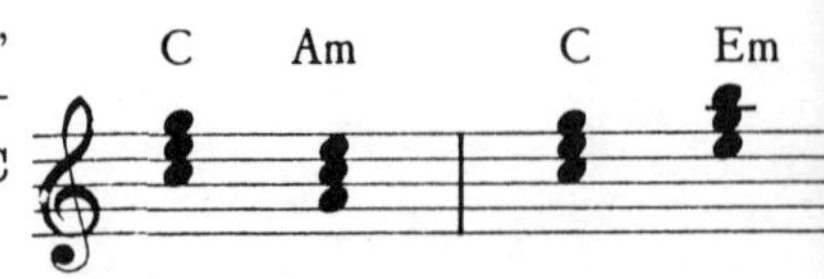

Since the Am and Em chords each share two notes with the C chord, they would be likely candidates to substitute for a C chord for variety. Since both the Am and Em are minor chords, they will create a different "flavor" than the C chord.

Here's a chart of chords that share two notes. These are all good candidates for substitutions.

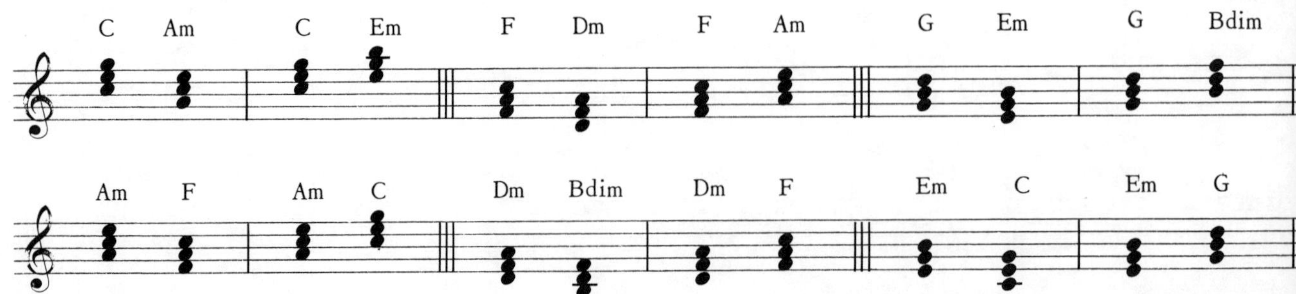

This arrangement of "The Water Kilpie" (from the Isle of Man) contains only Em and Am chords. This can get a bit boring. Try using "substitute chords" in SOME of the measures, instead. For example, you could change *some* of the Am chords to F or C chords, and change *some* of the Em chords to C or G chords. Also, remember that you can create variety by using inversions when you have the same chord repeated several times.

Experiment with substitute chords in this piece until you find the chords that you like. Write them in the music so you won't forget them. Then make your own arrangement of this beautiful and haunting piece.

THE WATER KILPIE

Chapter 21 - How To Figure Out Which Chords To Use

If you find a melody you like, but there are no chords indicated, how do you figure out which chords to play? There are several approaches to this problem.

I'd like to point out that there are no absolute "right" or "wrong" chords. Often there are several good choices. If 10 musicians figured out the chords for a particular piece, most of the chords would probably be the same in all 10 arrangements, but many of them would differ. If you like the sound of the chords, that is the most important criterion.

Also, be sure when you are figuring out chords that you do it in the context of the piece. For example, if you're trying to decide on a chord for the 4th measure, don't just play that one measure. Play the 3 preceding measures with the chords you picked, and then play the 4th measure, trying a possible chord. Then play all 4 measures again, trying a different possible chord on the 4th measure. This way, you can hear how the chord will sound in context, which may be very different than it sounds all by itself.

The first way you can try to figure out the chords is to use the I, IV and V chords we discussed in Chapter Eleven. For example, if you're in the key of C, your most common chords will be C (I), F (IV) and G (V). And so, on the first beat of every measure (or whenever you think the chords should change), you can try the 3 chords and decide which one you like best. By the way, 99% of all pieces in the key of C will begin and end on a C chord, so that's a good place to start.

Once you decide on which of the three chords you like in each measure, you can then consider changing some of them to "Substitute Chords", as we discussed in the previous chapter.

Another way to figure out your chords is to look at what notes are in each measure, and see if they form chords. For example, let's look at the Welsh song "One Morning in Springtime" on the next page.

In the first full measure the notes are C, G, and E . . . all of which are in a C chord. So, your obvious choice for that measure would be a C chord.

However, it isn't always that easy. When you have notes in a measure that don't fit into a logical chord, you need to decide which notes are the most important. There are some generalizations that we can make that are good guidelines. They may not always be true, but they're a good place to start:

1. The first beat of the measure is the strongest note, and should be part of the chord.
2. If you're in 4/4 time, the third beat is the next most important note. Sometimes you may want to change chords on this beat.
3. Longer notes are more important than short notes.
4. If there are eighth notes, the ones that fall on the beats are more important than the ones that fall on the off-beats (the "ands").

So now let's look at the 2nd measure of "One Morning in Springtime". The notes in are C, D, and E, but there is no chord that has all three of these notes in it. Going by rules #1 and #3 above, we can decide that the least important note in this measure is the D, since it is not the first beat, and is the shortest note. That leaves us with C and E notes, which are contained in a C chord, or an Am chord. So, your main choices for this measure would be either C or Am, depending on which one you like the sound of in this context.

Now on to measure 3. F, A and D are all contained in a Dm chord, so that would be a good choice. Another chord you might try would be an F chord, since it is one of the main chords in the key of C, and the first two notes of the measure are in an F chord. So, try a Dm and try an F, and see which one you like best.

Measure 4 has B and G notes, so your most likely chords would be G or Em, both of which contain hese two notes. Measure 5 is the same as the first measure, with notes from a C chord. In measure the F and the A are the most important notes, so your most likely choice would be an F chord, or erhaps a Dm.

The 7th measure gives you several choices. The notes are G, C, and B. You could use a G chord hroughout the measure (assuming that the C note isn't important). Or, you could start with a C hord for the first two beats (during the G and C notes in the melody), and then change to a G chord n the B note on the third beat. Then the 8th measure would be back to a C chord.

Continue in this manner throughout the piece, writing down which chords you like best in each easure. Remember that you can change chords within the measure if you'd like.

NE MORNING IN SPRINGTIME

Let's try to arrange "My Love She's But A Lassie Yet" using only our I, IV, and V chords (C, F, ar G). We can also use the G7 chord, since that is the most common 7th chord. In this piece, you'll ofte want to change chords halfway through the measure. For example, let's look at the 3rd line. Tl first two notes (G and E) would be a C chord. The next two notes (F and D) are part of a G7 chord. Tl next measure would be a C chord all the way through. The 3rd measure of that line starts with a chord (for the G and E notes). But the last half of the measure is a bit strange, with an F note and a E note. We could try another G7 (which has an F), or an F chord. I vote for an F chord, since we' want to go to a G or a G7 in the next measure.

Look at the last two measures of the piece. The very last measure will be a C chord (since mo pieces in the key of C end on a C chord, and the only notes in the measure are C's). However, tl next-to-the-last measure gives us lots of choices. The four sixteenth notes could either be a C chor (making the C and G notes of the melody the most important), or an F chord (emphasizing the C ar A notes). The next note (A) would be an F chord, and the last note of the measure (B) would be a chord. So, as I see it, here are your most likely candidates for those last two measures:

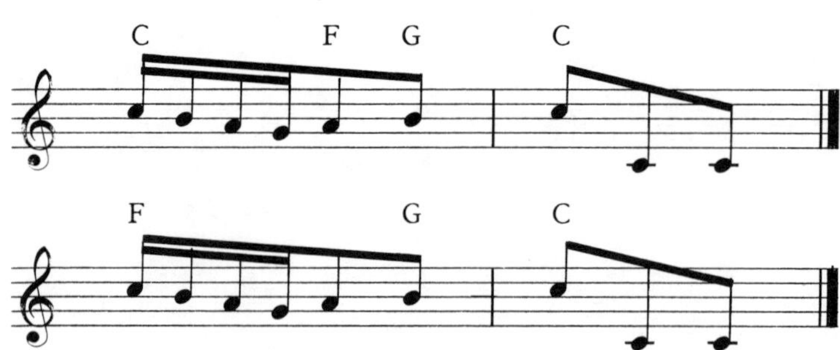

Figure out the rest of the chords for this piece, and make up an arrangement. It should be nice ar lively.

MY LOVE SHE'S BUT A LASSIE YET

Sometimes you want to figure out a chord to harmonize with just one note in the melody, instead of looking at the whole measure. To do this, you need to be able to think of what chords contain that one note. For example, let's say that the melody note is a C. What three chords contain a C note? The answer is a C chord, an Am chord, and an F chord.

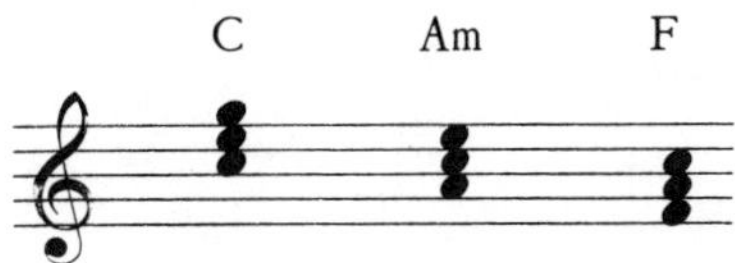

Therefore, you could try all these three chords in the context of the piece, and decide which one you like best.

One more example would be a melody note of a G. Which three chords are your most likely candidates, because they contain a G note?

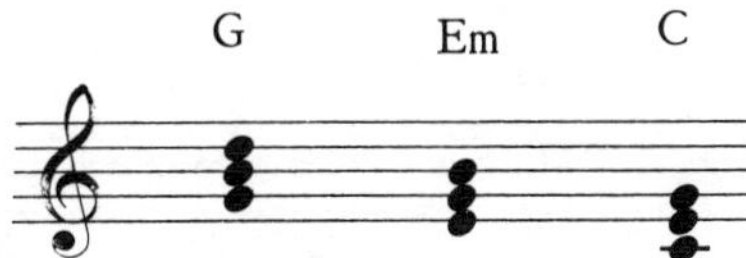

Play these next two versions of the Scottish song "I Know Where I'm Going". Notice how you can change the sound of the piece by putting more than one chord in each measure. The first version sounds fine, but the second version has more variety and depth. If the chords are going by really fast, you don't necessarily have to play all the notes in the extra chords. You can just "hint at them" by playing one or two notes or make them part of a countermelody.

I KNOW WHERE I'M GOING - VERSION #1

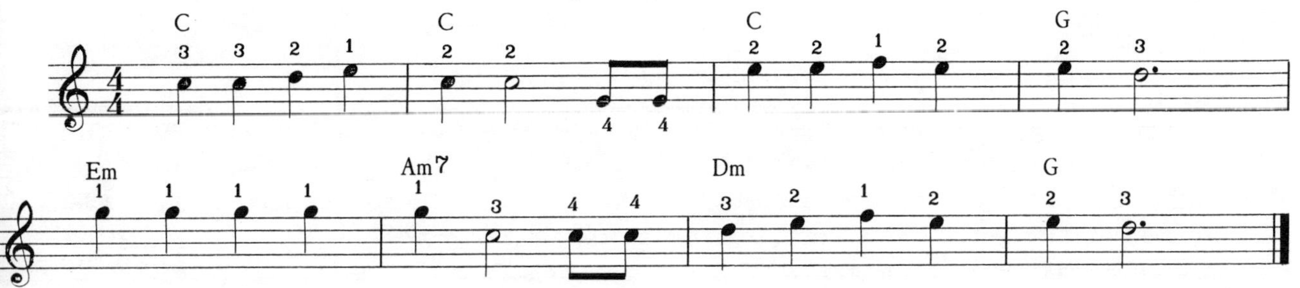

I KNOW WHERE I'M GOING - VERSION #2

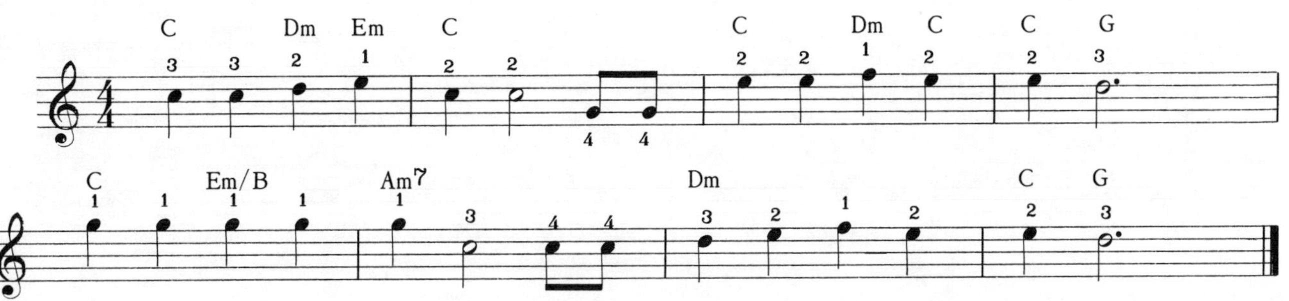

The concept of "hinting at chords" by playing just one or two notes, can be seen in my arrangement of the Irish tune "The Bells of Shandon". First of all, figure out your own chords using the first version of this piece below. You may want to change chords on the third beat of some of the measures as well as the first beat. Write down the chords that you like.

THE BELLS OF SHANDON - VERSION #1

Now look at the following arrangement of this piece. Go through the left hand and figure out what chords I used. Next, one measure at a time, look at the notes that I put on the third beat. Are they the same chord as I used on the first two beats? Do they "hint" at another chord, especially if you listen to the right and left hands together on that third beat?

Remember that it doesn't matter if my chords are the same ones you chose in your original version. As long as the chords sound good in the context of the piece, that is all that counts.

BELLS OF SHANDON - VERSION #2

Figure out the chords on "The Canigou" (France), "Moreton Bay" (Australia), and "Londonderry Air" (also known as "Danny Boy"). Remember that you can put more than one chord in any measure. Be sure to try the various chord possibilities in the context of the piece, and decide which ones you like.

THE CANIGOU

MORETON BAY

LONDONDERRY AIR or DANNY BOY

Chapter 22 - Irish Dance Tunes

When playing fast dance tunes, such as Irish jigs, reels, and hornpipes, you don't always have a lot of time to get all the notes of the chords in. When playing a complete chord on one beat, you usually have to play all the notes at once, instead of slightly breaking them as you normally do with chords of three or more notes. Also, the rhythm is extremely important in dance tunes, and so you want to emphasize the important beats with your accompaniment.

We'll go through the four main types of Irish dance tunes, and I'll show you some of the accompaniment patterns that I have found useful. Further information on these tunes can be found in my book "Irish Dance Tunes For All Harps".

Jigs are in 6/8 time, with an emphasis on beats 1 and 4. The basic accompaniment rhythms (which each take up three beats, or half of the measure) are: (a) a dotted quarter note, (b) a quarter and an eighth note, (c) three eighth notes. These three rhythms can be put together in various ways to make up a full measure. Here are some of the possibilities with the same chord throughout the measure. (I'm using a D chord for the examples in this chapter, since that is the key that many of these tunes are in.) Try some of these patterns in "Jackson's Fancy" and "Behind the Haystack". Don't forget that you can change chords halfway through the measure if you need to. Also, try experimenting with some short countermelodies every once in a while.

BEHIND THE HAYSTACK

Slip jigs are in 9/8 time, with emphasis on beats 1, 4, and 7. They use the same basic patterns as the jigs in 6/8 time, except there are three groups of 3 beats each instead of two. You still have the same basic rhythms: (a) a dotted quarter note, (b) a quarter and an eighth note, (c) three eighth notes. But in a slip jig you'd need three of these rhythms to make up a full measure instead of only two.

Try playing these slip jigs: "Ride A Mile Jig" and "Whinny Hills of Leitrim".

RIDE A MILE JIG

WHINNY HILLS OF LEITRIM

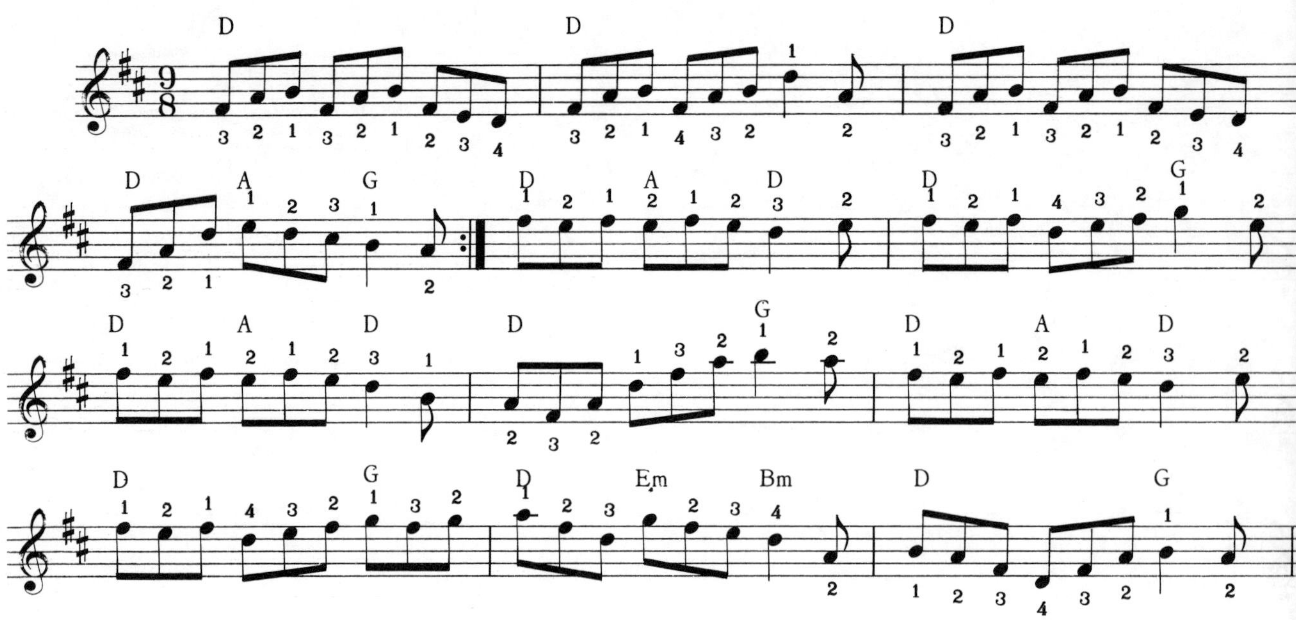

Reels are written in either 4/4 or cut time, with emphasis on beats 1 and 3. Hornpipes are also in 4/4 or cut time but are played slower than reels and have a bouncing dotted lilt to them. Although the melody rhythms are different in reels and hornpipes, their basic accompaniment rhythms are the same. The main left-hand rhythms are: (a) quarter notes, (b) half notes, (c) eighth notes. Since the tunes are so fast, I tend to use a lot more quarter and half notes, and fewer eighth notes. Here are some suggestions for accompaniment patterns for reels and hornpipes. Try these on "Reddigan's Reel" and "Lady Walpole's Reel", and on the two hornpipes: "Byrne's Hornpipe" and "Bantry Bay". When you need to change chords in the middle of a measure, just use half of the accompaniment pattern for each chord. Once again, these are only some of the possible patterns you can use.

REDDIGAN'S REEL

LADY WALPOLE'S REEL

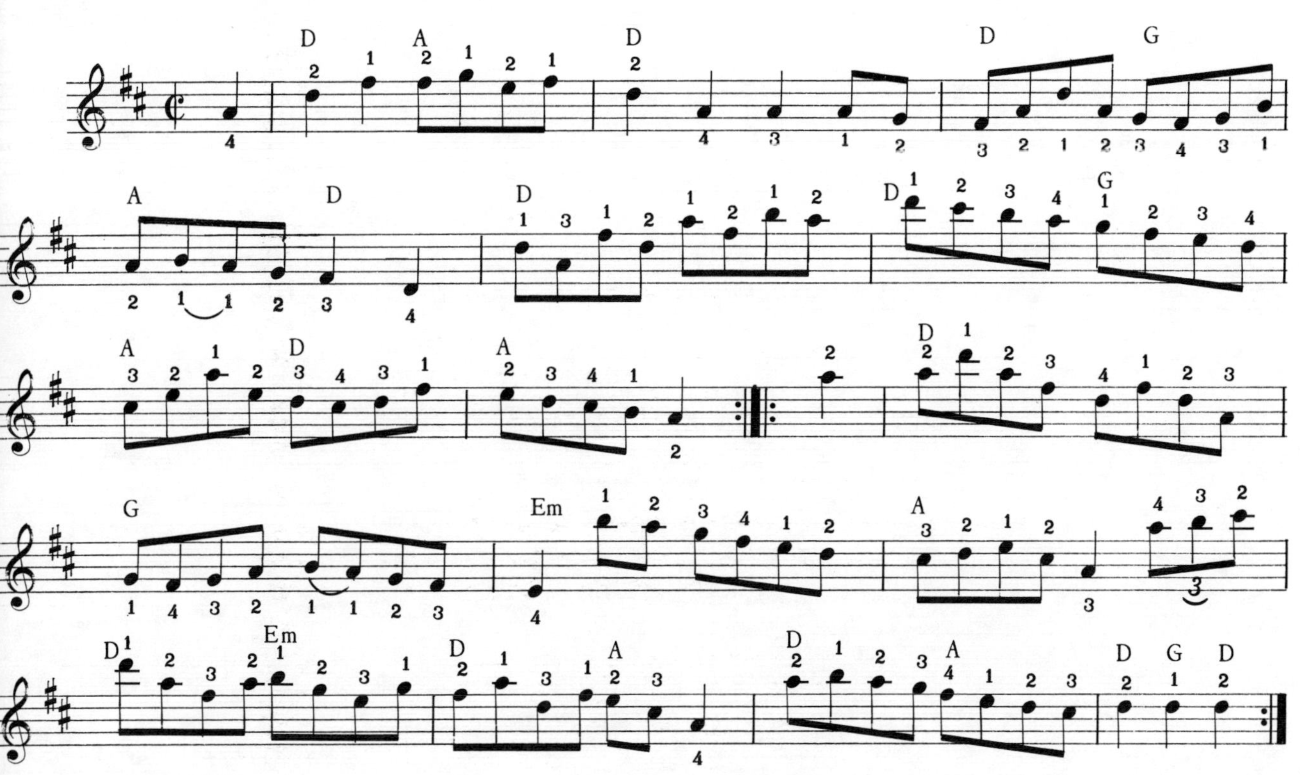

BYRNE'S HORNPIPE
BANTRY BAY

Chapter 23 - Vocal Arranging

Sometimes you may want to accompany a melody instrument or a vocalist (either yourself or someone else). This type of accompanying is very similar to the arranging we have done throughout this book. In fact, you can generally use the exact same arrangements that you have already figured out.

However, since the melody will be played or sung by the soloist, you don't necessarily have to play the melody on the harp. If you leave out the melody it will free up your right hand, and allow you to do some different things with your accompaniment. For example, you can now more easily play long arpeggios. Try these two patterns:

Now look at some of the patterns that you already know, and see how you can change them into two-handed patterns. Perhaps you can play the same pattern with both hands; or start the pattern on a different inversion with your right hand; or lengthen the pattern to fit with the two hands; or play one pattern with your right and a different one with your left, etc. Another idea is to play a countermelody with your right hand, along with your regular left-hand accompaniment.

If the song has lots of verses, you may want to use a different accompaniment for each one. Pay attention to what the words are saying, and try to match your playing to the various moods.

Chapter 24 - Transposing

Transposing means taking a piece that is in one key, and changing it into another key. This is very useful if your harp is tuned to the key of C, and you find a piece you like that is in the key of F, and you don't want to have to re-tune your harp.

Transposing will not eliminate accidentals; it only affects the sharps or flats in the key signature. For example, if throughout the piece one note is sometimes sharp and other times natural, transposing the piece into another key will not solve your problem. You'll still end up with accidentals, and will need to use your sharping levers for those notes.

Transposing is a subject that often scares people. But don't worry, it is really very easy. You just have to be able to (1) count up to 7, and (2) know how many sharps and flats are in each key. To help you with (2), I will reprint the key chart below.

NO. OF SHARPS	MAJOR KEY	NO. OF FLATS	MAJOR KEY
0	C	0	C
1	G	1	F
2	D	2	B♭
3	A	3	E♭
4	E	4	A♭
5	B	5	D♭
6	F#	6	G♭
7	C#	7	C♭

We'll now take some easy tunes and learn how to transpose them into the key of C. We'll start with Row, Row, Row Your Boat.

ROW, ROW, ROW YOUR BOAT

1. Our first step is to figure out what key the piece is in to start with. If you look at the beginning of the piece you'll see 2 sharps. Our chart above tells us that it must be in the key of D.

2. Next, we need to decide what key we want to transpose into. For our purposes now, we'll just transpose into the key of C. On the blank staff on the top of the next page, write in the NEW key signature. Since the key of C has no sharps or flats, leave it blank.

3. We now know that we want to go from the key of D to the key of C. What is the interval from D up to C? Remember how we figured out intervals before? Starting with D as number 1, count how many strings there are on your harp from D to C: D=1, E=2, F=3, G=4, A=5, B=6, C=7. So, from D to C (counting both the D and the C) is an interval of a 7th. Therefore, if we raise every note in the original piece up a 7th, and we have the correct key signature, we'll AUTOMATICALLY have transposed the piece into the key of C. Let's try it. Write the notes on the staff on the top of the next page.

The first note is D, so by going up a 7th, the note in the NEW piece will be C (an octave above middle C). Write in that note as a dotted quarter note, just like the original. The next two notes, of course, will be C's as well, since the first three notes in the original are the same pitch. Write them down with the same timing as the original (another dotted quarter, a bar line, and a quarter note). The next note in the original version was an E. An interval of a 7th up from E is . . . D. So, the next note you'll write down is a quarter note D (one above the first three C notes).

Continue in this manner, going up a 7th for each note, until you have completed transposing the piece.

Now, be sure your harp is in the key of C (no sharps or flats), and play the new version of "Row, Row, Row Your Boat" that you have just created. It should sound correct. If some of the notes sound funny, you didn't move all the notes up a 7th. Count them all again. It should sound just like the "Row Row Row" you've always known and loved. (If you're still stuck, you can check my version in the appendix.)

If it sounded right, congratulations! You've now transposed your first piece. Now that you've done it, I'm going to show you a short cut for that one. To figure out how far we should move the notes when we transposed this piece, we counted from the key of D UP to C, and came up with an interval of a 7th. However, we could have counted DOWN instead of UP. Let's try that. How far is it from D DOWN to C? Counting both the D and the C (as we always do when figuring out intervals) it is a 2nd. Or, in other words, just move every note down ONE string. (Yes, an interval of a 2nd is only one string away. Think about it.)

Boy, going down one string sure sounds easier than counting up an interval of a 7th doesn't it! So, now, let's try it again. On the blank staves below, transpose "Row, Row, Row" from the original key of D again to the key of C . . . this time, just moving each note DOWN ONE STRING.

How did you do? Play this version and see if it sounds like your old favorite. It should look just like the first one you wrote out, except an octave lower. (If you're still confused, read the instructions again, and check my version in the appendix.)

OK. Now let's try another piece. I'm sure this is another one of your all-time-favorites: "London Bridge is Falling Down".

LONDON BRIDGE IS FALLING DOWN

1. What key is the piece currently in? The correct answer is E♭ .
2. We're going to transpose this piece into the key of C, which has no sharps or flats, so we don't need to put any sharps or flats in our new key signature . . . we'll just leave it blank.
3. What is the interval between E♭ and C. If we count DOWN, it is a third. (For purposes of transposing, we don't care if it is a major third, or a minor third. If we set our key signatures correctly, they will take care of everything. So, all we have to know is that it is a 3rd.) If we count UP, instead, from E♭ to C, we come up with a 6th. It seems to me that it will be easier to count down a 3rd than it is to count up a 6th, so that's what we'll do.
4. On the staff below, transpose "London Bridge" into the key of C by moving each note down a 3rd. The easy, "shorthand" way of doing this is to move each note that is on a line down to the next line (i.e. the first note B♭ which is on the 3rd line of the staff, will move down to G, which is on the second line of the staff), and any note that is on a space will move down to the next space (i.e. the second note which is a C on the third space of the staff will now be an A on the second space).
5. After you've transposed the notes, you need to transpose the chord names as well. It is the same as transposing the notes. In this instance we've been moving DOWN a 3rd, so all the E♭ chords will now be C chords (down a 3rd), and the B♭ chords will also move down a 3rd to . . . G chords.
6. When you're finished, play the piece you've written out and see if it sounds ok. If so, you did great! If not, go back and figure out what you did wrong. If you need to, check my version in the appendix.

Now that you've gotten so good at transposing, let's transpose "London Bridge" into the Key of G. Follow the steps below, being sure you put one sharp (F#) in your new key signature. When you're finished, if you need help, check my version in the appendix. But be sure to try it yourself, first.

TRANSPOSING STEPS

1. Figure out what key the piece is currently written in. (Use the charts if necessary).

2. Decide what key you want to transpose the piece into. On your new manuscript paper, write t new key signature at the beginning of the piece. (If you're going into the key of C, this will blank.)

3. Figure out the interval from the name of the original key to the name of the new key. You c count either up or down, depending on which one is closer or easier.

4. Move each note up (or down) that number of strings. Be sure that if you count UP in step #3 th you go UP in this step; and if you count DOWN in step #3 that you go DOWN in this step. Otherwi you'll be in big trouble!

5. Transpose the chords the same way by moving them the same interval and the same direction y decided on in step #3.

6. Play the piece and make sure it sounds correct.

Here is one more example for you to practice. Follow the 6 steps above, and transpose "Brahı Lullaby" into the key of C, and then also into the key of G. If you need help after you're finish check my versions in the appendix.

BRAHMS' LULLABY

Conclusion

Congratulations! You've made it through the book! Now you're ready to go out into the big wide world of music and tackle other pieces. You can buy guitar books, banjo books, piano books with chord indications, dulcimer books, fiddle books, etc. and make your own arrangements. The whole world of music is at your fingertips. Of course, many pieces will not be suitable for our folk harps, because of the problems we have with accidentals, so you'll need to pick your pieces carefully. But there is plenty of music out there that CAN be easily adapted to our beautiful instrument. Keep up the good work, and get out there and have fun!

Appendix

Page 18 - INTERVALS

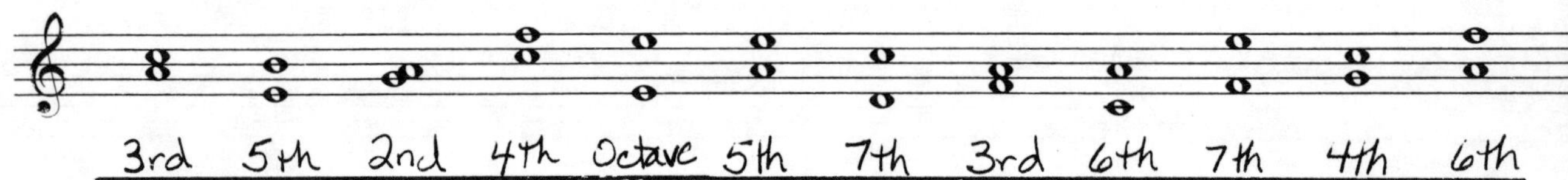

Page 20 - SHORTHAND NOTATION

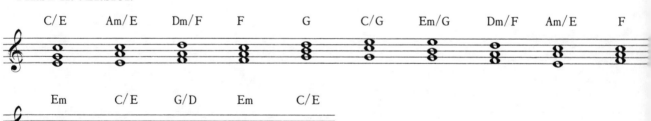

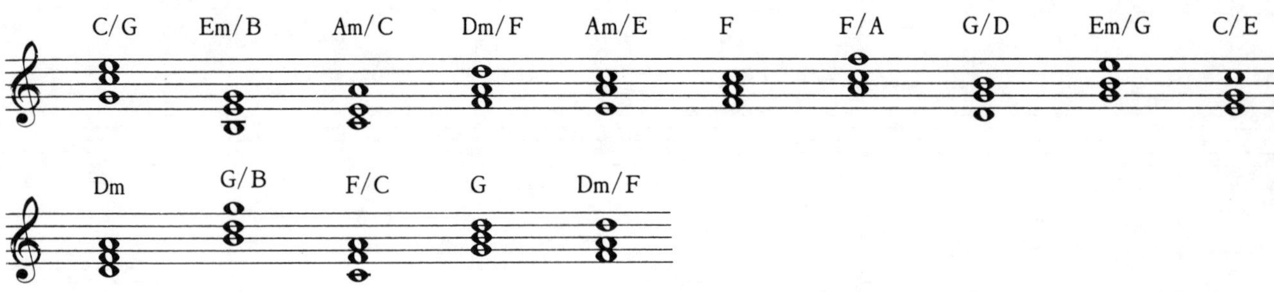

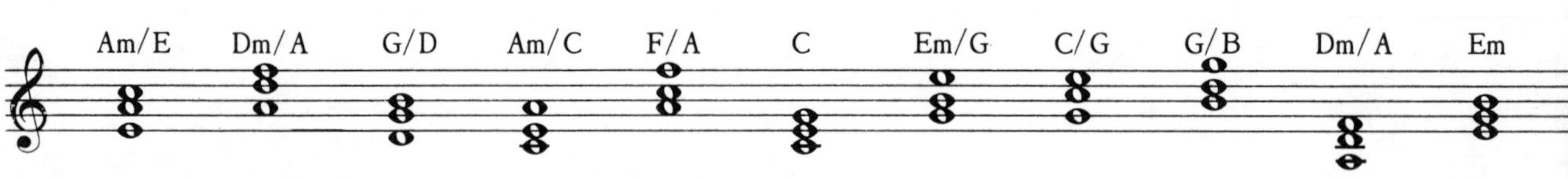

Am/C Em/B G C/E F/C

Page 30 - CLOSEST INVERSIONS

FIRST INVERSION

C/E Am/E Dm/F F G C/G Em/G Dm/F Am/E F

Em C/E G/D Em C/E

SECOND INVERSION

C/G Am Dm/A F/A G/B C Em/B Dm/A Am F/A

Em/G C/G G Em/G C/G

Page 35 - INTERVALS OF A 3rd

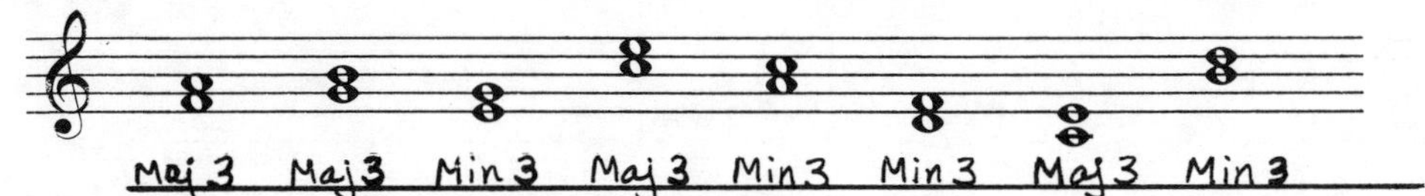

Page 40 - MAJOR KEY SIGNATURES

Page 40 - MINOR KEY SIGNATURES

Page 45 - I - IV - V

1. In the key of C
   the three major chords are: C F G
   the three minor chords are: Am Dm Em
   the diminished chord is: b dim.

2. In the key of G
   the three major chords are: G C D
   the three minor chords are: Em Am Bm
   the diminished chord is: F# dim.

3. In the key of A
   the three major chords are: A D E
   the three minor chords are: F#m Bm C#m
   the diminished chord is: G# dim.

4. In the key of D
   the three major chords are: D G A
   the three minor chords are: Bm Em F#m
   the diminished chord is: C# dim.

5. In the key of F
   the three major chords are: F Bb C
   the three minor chords are: Dm Gm Am
   the diminished chord is: E dim.

6. In the key of Bb
   the three major chords are: Bb Eb F
   the three minor chords are: Gm Cm Dm
   the diminished chord is: A dim.

Page 101 - ROW, ROW, ROW YOUR BOAT - KEY OF C #1

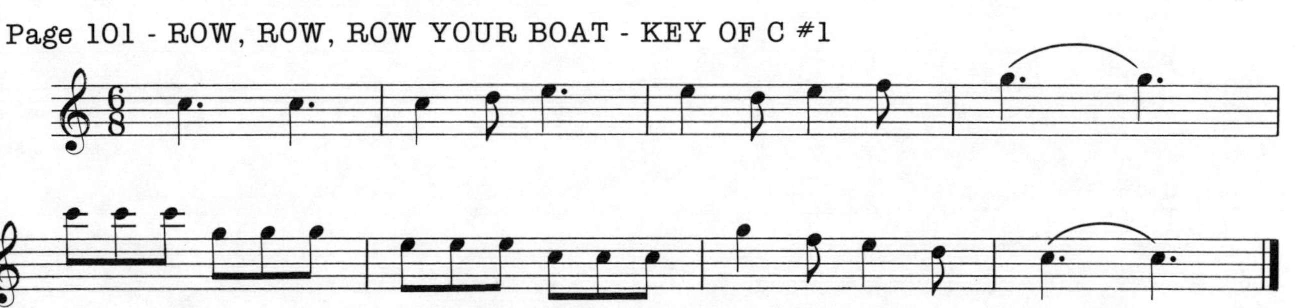

Page 101 - ROW, ROW, ROW YOUR BOAT - KEY OF C #2

Page 102 - LONDON BRIDGE IS FALLING DOWN - KEY OF C

Page 102 - LONDON BRIDGE IS FALLING DOWN - KEY OF G

Page 104 - BRAHM'S LULLABY - KEY OF C

Page 104 - BRAHM'S LULLABY - KEY OF G

Alphabetical Index Of Tunes